DIALOGUES IN BLACK HISTORY

DIALOGUES IN BLACK HISTORY

by
ROBERT A. STOVALL

VANTAGE PRESS
New York   Washington   Atlanta   Hollywood

FIRST EDITION

*All rights reserved, including the right
of reproduction in whole or part in any form.*

Copyright © 1976 by Robert A. Stovall

Published by Vantage Press, Inc.
516 West 34th Street, New York, New York 10001

Printed in the United States of America

Standard Book Number 533-02257-6

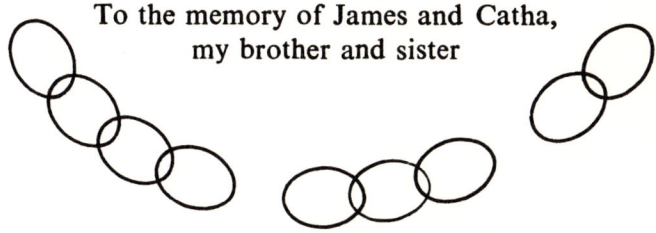

To the memory of James and Catha,
my brother and sister

CONTENTS

Preface

1	Slavery in Other Lands	1
2	Slavery in the West Indies	11
3	Slavery in the Colonies	21
4	Geography and Slavery	29
5	Did Slaves Dare Revolt?	39
6	Slave Revolts in the 1800s	51
7	Abolitionists—Part I	63
8	Abolitionists—Part II	69
9	The Prelude to the Civil War	81
10	Black People and the Civil War Years	91
11	The Black Man and Reconstruction	99
12	Economics, Education and Reconstruction	107
13	Black People and the Supreme Court	113
14	A Final Word	123

PREFACE

While teaching social studies in the inner-city schools, I have become deeply aware of the lack of interest on the part of students as they attempt to relate to the rather prosaic manner in which many of our social studies texts are written. Since reading is one of the major problems in the inner-city school, surely we must do more to motivate the development of this very basic skill. I believe this can be accomplished much more effectively if we can increase the stimulus value of our subject matter, particularly in the area of social studies.

One of the main purposes of this book is to try and make history live as a more relevant discipline, especially for the inner-city child. With this objective in mind, I have taken into consideration the cognitive as well as the affective learning styles of the inner-city child. The affective dimensions of this book are expressed rather poignantly by the intermittent use of colloquial expressions which I have found to be highly functional in the vocabulary of the inner-city child.

The contents of this book includes selective topics on the black experience, from the early African slave trade to the 1954 Supreme Court decision on segregated schools. However, I should hasten to add that this book is not designed to be a definitive study of the black experience in America; but may be used most effectively as a supplement to an American history text. As the title suggests, this book is written in dialogue and can easily be adapted for use as historical drama.

In addition to being used as a social studies supplement, the English teacher, as well as the drama teacher, may find this book very useful in their classrooms.

As these dialogues are read, one will surely become aware of the moral underpinnings. This, of course, is not by accident. In my opinion, the social and moral crises of our time calls for a curriculum that can inspire the development of character, as well as instruct the intellect. In other words, moral education, founded on humanistic values, must become an integral part of the curriculum as basic subject matter.

Finally, I owe thanks to many of my former students who directly and indirectly inspired many of the questions and comments that are developed in the following dialogues. Also, I extend my profound gratitude to my wife, Adelyn, for her inspiration and helpful suggestions.

DIALOGUES IN BLACK HISTORY

Chapter 1

SLAVERY IN OTHER LANDS

Persons of the Dialogue: Teacher, Sha, Janet, Darryl, Yogi, Bob, Joe, and Teddy.

> *... Sometimes beating them with the burning passions of greed and selfishness, but always reducing them to something less than their human potential ...*

TEACHER: Today we will begin our study of slavery. Our primary concern will be on slavery in America. However, I believe it is important that we understand that slavery is not unique to the American experience.

SHA: Teacher, are you suggesting that slavery existed in other societies before Black people were imported from Africa to America in the early 1500s?

TEACHER: Yes, I think it is very important that we understand that slavery, in one form or another, has existed in most previous societies and civilizations. However, slavery, as an institution, did not always manifest itself in the same pattern in past societies.

JANET: Why is it that only Black people were made slaves?

SHA: Janet, you are wrong in assuming that only Black people were made slaves in the past. According to history, enslavement could be, and was often, the fate of any person, regardless of the color of their skin.

TEACHER: You are absolutely correct, Sha; among the early Greeks and Romans, as well as other ancient societies, the color of one's skin did not prevent him from being taken into slavery. As a matter of fact, whites enslaved whites by the millions in past societies.

DARRYL: You just said that whites enslaved each other in Roman and Greek societies, as well as other ancient societies. My question is, was this also true in Africa—that is, did Africans enslave each other?

TEACHER: Indeed they did. As a matter of fact, slavery, in one form or another, had very deep roots in many parts of Africa long before the transatlantic slave trade was initiated by Europeans in the early sixteenth century.

YOGI: Are there historical records which would indicate when men first began to enslave each other.

TEACHER: Yogi, you have to understand that in early ancient civilizations, they didn't always keep very accurate records. However, there is evidence to suggest that slavery existed in Egypt as early as 2600 B.C. There is also reliable evidence that slavery existed in ancient Babylonia, Assyria, and as I have already suggested, ancient Rome and Greece.

BOB: You know, I find it very difficult to understand why one man would want to enslave another man. The whole idea seems so inconsistent with the laws of nature.

JAN: What do you mean—inconsistent with the laws of nature? You always try to use those big words.

BOB: The only thing big about what I said is the "truth."

JAN: Now you are trying to be philosophical.

BOB: Be that as it may—my point is this: Since we all share a common humanity—why would one man force another man to serve him against his will. To me, the whole idea seems very repulsive.

DARRYL: Teacher, you know, Bob comes on like one of those "home boy" philosophers. If he had some eye glasses setting upon his nose, he would fit the description in every sense of the the word.

TEACHER: I think Bob's point is very well taken, and I am inclined to agree with him. However, before we go further, I should like to point out some of the ways and reasons people were taken into slavery in ancient societies. In past societies slavery took place in many different ways. Many people were forced into slavery as a result of capture in warfare, as punishment for some criminal act or because of one's inability to pay a debt that he owed. In addition to what we just said, some people sold themselves or members of their families into slavery as a means of paying their debts or meeting some other very pressing obligation. What I have just described, of course, was called voluntary slavery.

BOB: Are you suggesting that people would sometimes give up their children or their own freedom in order that a debt should be paid?

TEACHER: Yes, Bob, this was a very common practice among some early ancient societies.

BOB: Well, I guess man has always been immoral.

TEACHER: Perhaps you are right. However, I must remind you that the enslavement of human beings was not always considered immoral by people of the past. The enslavement of human beings, as I have suggested, was very widespread in ancient societies, and anyone, regardless of his race, creed or color, ran the risk of being enslaved if he was at the wrong place at the wrong time.

JANET: Is it true that slaves were always outsiders?

TEACHER: What do you mean Janet?

JANET: For example, Romans didn't enslave Romans, Greeks didn't enslave Greeks—but instead, they enslaved people who were usually thought of as foreigners or outsiders.

TEACHER: Yes, Janet, you are quite right. As a matter of fact, early Roman law explicitly stated that if a Roman was to be enslaved as a punishment—he had to be sold abroad. Islamic law has always embraced the idea that a person born a Muslim could not be enslaved by another Muslim. This same pattern was followed by most societies where slavery was practiced.

SHA: You said earlier that slavery was deeply rooted in African history just as it was in other ancient societies. Will you please elaborate on that statement? I am particularly interested in knowing more about slavery in West Africa.

TEACHER: Why West Africa?

SHA: Because that's where most of our ancestors came from; and I want to know more about it.

JOE: You say that with such a deep sense of pride.

SHA: Why should I not speak of Africa with a deep sense of pride. After all, West Africa has a long and interesting history. She has given birth to a number of highly developed civilizations including Mali, Ghana and Songhay—not to mention Egypt in North Africa; which many have spoken of as the cradle of civilization.

JOE: But you see, that's not the way I heard it.

SHA: Then, tell me, brother, how did you hear it?

JOE: I heard that Africa was a land of lions and jungles.

SHA: You know what, brother, you are a victim of too many Tarzan movies. You need to get away from that tube and dig into your history. Because in the first place, lions don't live in jungles, and secondly, only five percent of Africa can be considered as jungles.

JOE: You said I should dig into my history. I am not sure that I know what you mean. Because, as I see it, my history begins and ends right here in America. I have no roots in Africa. My roots were plucked from African soil more than three hundred years ago. I am certainly not proud of this—but that's the way it is.

SHA: If indeed that is the extent of your understanding—the gods of fate have dealt most unjustly with you; and nothing short of wisdom and knowledge can free you from such a short-sighted attitude in regards to your place in history.

JOE: Perhaps you are right—however, I am not looking back to Africa, I must deal with the realities of the present situation; because this is the only reality that I know.

SHA: Did it ever occur to you that it is extremely difficult to understand your present situation before you have come face-to-face with your past. Very few people have made this evasion successfully.

TEACHER: The dialogue between the two of you is indeed interesting. However, as I recall, Sharon asked me to elaborate further on slavery in West Africa. Therefore, let me speak on that before we go further. The status of a slave in West Africa was undoubtedly the lowest of a number of social levels. Slaves were usually very dependent upon their masters and were usually required to do the most undesirable kinds of work. As in other ancient societies, in West Africa one could be enslaved for nonpayment of a debt or for committing a crime. However, most slaves in West Africa were captives of war. By this, I mean that from time to time, different tribes would engage each other in war and the tribe winning the war would enslave members of the other tribe.

SHA: Did they enslave them for life as was done later in America?

TEACHER: No, as we shall see, slavery in Africa was quite different from slavery in America. While slaves occupied the lowest social class in West Africa, they were usually not dehumanized as they were later in America.

SHA: Am I correct in assuming that the status of slavery was not inherited in Africa as it was in America?

TEACHER: You are correct.

SHA: Why do you think the status of slavery was not inherited in Africa?

TEACHER: Perhaps this can be traced to their view of slavery. Africans did not view slaves as being inferior human beings —to them a slave was a victim of circumstances, usually, a captive of war. I might add that in Africa, slaves often married into their master's family and became equal members of the household. This, of course, would tend to suggest that there was no lasting stigma attached to being a slave in Africa.

DARRYL: You just said that most slaves in Africa were captives of war. My question is, when slaves were taken as captives of war, were they usually sold or did they just serve as slaves for those who captured them?

TEACHER: Good question. In early Africa slaves were not bought or sold. As a matter of fact, slaves were not bought and sold in West Africa until the Arabic influence begin to spread throughout West Africa about the twelfth century. During this same period, the Arabs introduced the Cowrie shells which were used as currency or money. The use of the Cowrie shells as money greatly facilitated the trading process. Once West Africa had developed a system of money, this greatly accelerated the exportation of slaves to other countries of Islamic influence.

SHA: Is it safe to conclude that slavery in West Africa, to some extent, was similar to the feudal system of medieval Europe? It seems that the more I read about serfdom and vassalship during the Middle Ages in Western Europe, the greater the similarities become.

TEACHER: Very good observation. The medieval states of Africa clearly show how close the condition of subjugated people in Africa was to that of the feudal vassals in Europe. For example, in the Songhay kingdom of the fifteenth century, along the Middle Niger, non-Muslim people of the forest were used extensively in agriculture. Like the serfs of Europe, they were settled on the land and tied to it. In return for using the land, they paid tribute to their masters in crops, as well as personal services. This system, however, had very limited usage in Africa. Generally speaking, slavery in Africa was domestic in nature. In other words, most of the slaves were household servants, and not tillers of the soil.

TEDDY: You may have answered this question before; however, it is not clear in my mind, therefore, I will ask it again. Were African slaves sold to foreign countries before the Euro-American slave trade began in the early 1500s?

TEACHER: Yes, as I attempted to indicate before, slave trading of Africans to foreign countries began many years before the Euro-American slave trade begin in the 1500s. Prior to this time, African slaves were taken to Persia, Arabia and other lands under Islamic control.

TEDDY: In other words, the Islamic societies were among the first to transport human cargo from Africa to foreign countries?

TEACHER: This would seem to be the case; especially in the Sudan region. I think there is sufficient evidence to suggest that some Islamic societies were exporting slaves from the Sudan region of Africa as early as the twelfth century. Some historians suggest that this foreign trade may have started as early as the eleventh century.

TEDDY: Very well, I understand.

TEACHER: Obviously, we could go on and on discussing slavery in Africa and other parts of the world. However, to do so would prevent us from discussing one of our primary concerns—slavery in America. If there are no additional comments or burning words of wisdom, I suggest that we cross the Atlantic and begin our discussion of slavery in America.

BOB: Before we leave our discussion of Africa, I have a final word.

TEACHER: Speak.

BOB: As I sit here looking back upon the historical evolution of men and societies, I can see more clearly how slavery has raised its ugly head and entered the affairs of men—sometimes beating them with the burning passions of greed and selfishness, but always reducing them to something less than their human potential. In the final analysis, I think history should record that Mother Africa has given to the world, reluctantly, more than its share of human cargo—a fact that is indelibly written on the souls of Black people everywhere.

JANET: I just knew you wouldn't allow this dialogue to end without interjecting some burning words of wisdom. However, I can personally attest to the truth of what you have said. In other words, I know the direction in which you are pointing.

TEACHER: However undesirable slavery may have been, its history dates back to the ancient civilizations of early man. As we shall see, nations have flourished on the backs of slaves, and at the same time, nations have stood in fear and turmoil as a result of the tension generated by slaves and those freemen who stood up and spoke out against it. In the following pages of these dialogues, it may be possible to show that the effects of slavery are still resounding throughout the Western world.

Discussion Questions

1. What is meant by the statement "slaves were usually outsiders"?
2. How was slavery in Africa different from slavery in America?
3. Give at least three reasons as to why people were enslaved in ancient societies.
4. How was slavery in West Africa similar to the feudal system of medieval Europe?
5. Were African Slaves sold to foreign countries before the Euro-American slave trade begin? Explain.

Words you should know:

ancient
transatlantic

initiate
immoral
Islamic
civilizations
dehumanize
subjugate
feudal
vassals
medieval
historian
turmoil

Chapter 2

SLAVERY IN THE WEST INDIES

Persons of the Dialogue: Teacher, Kevin, Tammie, Tony, Angie, Michelle, Janet, Regie, Yogi, Lisa, Lynn, Darryl, and Joe.

> *... Why me, why me, why was I chosen to bear the cross of slavery, while other men went free ...*

TEACHER: In the previous dialogue, we said that in one form or another, slavery had existed in most ancient societies. We also said that slavery in ancient civilizations was not the burden of any particular race of people. Anyone, white, black or brown, at the wrong place at the wrong time, ran the risk of being taken into slavery. As we shall see, this was not the case in America.

KEVIN: You just said that in ancient societies slavery was not the burden of any particular race of people. It could happen to anyone who was at the wrong place at the wrong time. Now, if that was the situation in ancient societies, why is it that all of a sudden only Black people were being enslaved in America. Why did this have to happen to Black people? There were white people here, and there were the Indians who had been in America for thousands of years — why weren't they enslaved?

TEACHER: You have raised a good point. Let's see if we can answer that. A few years after Columbus had discovered the Indians in the West Indies, he attempted to enslave them. As a matter of fact, when Columbus returned to Spain in 1495, he and his men took 1100 Indians as slaves. However, when the ship arrived in Spain, only some 300 of the Indians were alive; and most of them soon died.

KEVIN: You just said that Columbus took Indians to Spain as slaves. My question is, why didn't they use Indians as slaves in America?

TAMMIE: Kevin, in the early years of the Spanish conquest of Hispaniola, the Indians were forced into slavery.

TEACHER: You are right, Tammie—shortly after Columbus conquered the Tainos Indians of Hispaniola, he began to levy tributes upon them. This, of course, was the beginning of the encomiendas that forced the Indians to do slave labor.

TONY: What were encomiendas?

TEACHER: The encomiendas was a system or plan set up by Columbus which gave the Spanish soldiers and colonists tracts of land or villages to use for their own benefit. This plan also gave the soldiers and colonists the right to force Indians to work for them.

MICHELLE: What kind of work were the Indians required to do?

ANGIE: Believe it or not—they forced the Indians to extract gold from the gold dust of the river beds. The work of the Indians was made extremely difficult because they were required to produce a certain amount of gold every three months. The Indians became so bitter and displeased with their situation as slaves that many ran away and others revolted.

KEVIN: I hear you, but I am wondering, what did Columbus and those other dudes do to those Indians who revolted and ran away. In other words, how did they deal with this?

ANGIE: Well, when they ran away, first of all, they had to try and catch them. They used hound dogs to try and track them down. If the hound dogs were successful in tracking them down, they were usually returned and punished severely. However, let there be no mistake about it: thousands of Indians were so determined that they would not be slaves, that they took poison to hasten their escape to the land of the dead, where neither dogs nor slave drivers could pursue them and put them in chains again.

TEACHER: You are quite right, Angie, in your analysis of the Indian's attitude toward slavery. Perhaps I can add to our discussion by giving you some population data on the Indians of Hispaniola. When Columbus came to America in 1492, it is estimated that he found 300,000 Indians living in Hispaniola. Within two years, approximately 100,000 Indians had been killed or had died for one reason or another. In 1508, some fifteen years after Columbus landed in Hispaniola, approximately 60,000 Indians were still alive. By 1548, Spanish records indicated that only 500 Indians, out of the original 300,000, were still alive in Hispaniola.

JANET: A terrible thing for sure. Earlier, someone said that the Indian men were forced to work in mines, usually fourteen hours a day; did the women also work in mines?

TEACHER: No, Janet, as a rule, only Indian men worked in the mines. As for the women, they were forced to do domestic and agricultural labor. However, as we shall see, Europeans were not very successful in their attempt to enslave the Indians.

REGIE: You just said that the Europeans were not very successful in their attempt to enslave the Indians—was this because the Indians refused to accept the burden of slavery?

TEACHER: Yes, that was partly the reason; however, there were also other reasons.

REGIE: What were some of the other reasons?

YOGI: I think I know some of the reasons.

TEACHER: Will you share them with us, Yogi?

YOGI: Only if you insist.

TEACHER: I insist.

YOGI: Well, you see, it was like this: When the white man came over from Europe to America, he brought some diseases that the Indians were not *hip* to; and as a result, many Indians became ill and died.

TEACHER: Yogi, when you say *hip*—you mean the Indians had not built up an immunity to many of the diseases brought over by Europeans?

YOGI: Well, if you want to put it like that—in essence, I think we are saying the same thing. However, to put it in technical terms, the Indians didn't have the antibodies needed for resisting the diseases brought over by the European white man.

TEACHER: Very well said.

TONY: Yes, Yogi just said that the Indians were not *hip* to some of the diseases brought over to America by the white man; if I may add to that—neither were they *hip* to the fourteen and fifteen hour workdays required of them by the Europeans. As a result, many of them ran away, others committed suicide, and still others fell beneath the weight of slavery as they attempted to bear the white man's burdens. The Indians were not accustomed to the heavy and trying work tasks imposed upon them by the white man; and most of them didn't put forth any effort to adjust.

REGIE: Why me—why me—why me—why was I chosen to bear the cross of slavery while other men went free?

TEACHER: You see, Reginald, it is a very long story—with more than four hundred years of history hehind it—but certainly, you are not the first Black to ask this question "why me," and in centuries to come, I am sure that this question will be raised again, again, and again. Perhaps no one will ever be able to answer that question to the satisfaction of many Blacks; however, let us look into the pages of history and see if we can throw some light on this most difficult question. Who will lead us?

LISA: I will try. First of all, I think we have to understand that one of the primary reasons for Europeans coming to America was to gain wealth. The mines and the plantations demanded production on a very large scale, as well as very cheap labor, if a profit was to be made. The Indians knew nothing of mine and plantation labor; and to put it in contemporary language, they just didn't "dig it"—and furthermore, they refused to do it. Of course, they got some help from nature, as well as some religious leaders.

KEVIN: Look, Lisa, I am very much aware of the role that nature played in relieving the Indians of their chains. However, I know nothing of religious leaders coming to the aid of the Indians. Speak, that I may hear the good news.

LISA: Yes, good for the Indians, but bad for Black people.

KEVIN: What do you mean?

LISA: This is what I mean: Bartolomé de Las Casas, the first priest to be ordained in America, developed a great deal of sympathy for the Indians and the inhumane way that they were being treated. As a result, he gave up his Indian slaves and began to speak out against the use of Indians as slaves.

KEVIN: A very courageous act.

LISA: Hear me out and then make your comments. At the same time that Bartolomé de Las Casas was preaching against enslaving the Indians, he was asking the King of Spain for permission to replace the Indians with African slaves. After making a number of trips to Spain, Las Casas finally convinced Charles V, the King of Spain, that Africans should replace the Indians as slaves in the New World.

LYNN: I am completely confused. On the one hand you say Las Casas was attacking the injustice of slavery against the Indians—at the same time, you said he was asking the King of Spain for permission to enslave Africans. Did he have something against Black people?

TEACHER: Las Casas, like many others, advocated the idea that Africans were physically stronger than Indians and, therefore, they were more able to endure the hard labor and the very hot climate.

LYNN: Well, that's some jutsification for replacing Indians with Africans. You know, the whole thing sounds like one big, highly contrived myth.

TEACHER: There is certainly no reliable evidence to support the above theory. For in time, surely others would have adjusted to the hot climate as well as the hard labor, in much the same way that the Africans adjusted. However, there are other reasons that appear to be more credible.

DARRYL: Yes, I have heard it all before.

TONY: Well, I am sure that many of us have not—so, will you share some of your information with us.

DARRYL: OK—this is one of the reasons they said Africans were more desirable as slaves than the Indians: Africans were supposed to have been more resistant to the white man's diseases—such as yellow fever, measles and malaria. If indeed this were the case, under these circumstances, you could expect Africans to be healthier, live longer and produce more. After all, the slave owners were only concerned about getting the greatest amount of work out of each human body.

TONY: Oh—I see, tell us more.

DARRYL: There were also those who contended that Africans could better adjust to the plantation system because they came from an economic system that was more advanced than that of the Indians.

TONY: Hey, man, they sure invented enough excuses to try and justify putting the Black man in those mines and on those plantations.

MICHELLE: For sure.

TEACHER: In my opinion, one can never morally justify slavery. However, there is, in my opinion, sufficient evidence to support the notion that Africans were more resistant to the white man's diseases than the Indians. Secondly, West Africans did come from a more advanced economic system than the Indians of Hispaniola.

KEVIN: There are still other reasons that Blacks were found to be more desirable as slaves than the Indians.

JOE: What did they say this time?

KEVIN: Well, many pointed to the notion that Africans were more desirable than the Indians because of their high visibility; and their limited knowledge of the geographical environment in which they were expected to live and work.

JOE: Hey, man, I don't understand a word that you said—now, would you please cut out the big words and speak in the tongue, so that we can understand where you are coming from.

KEVIN: What do you mean, Joe? I thought I was speaking English.

JOE: Yes, that's just the point. Have you ever tried speaking a little Ghetto English. There is a difference, you know.

KEVIN: I don't know how to say that in Ghetto English.

JOE: Oh, I forgot! you are one of those students who is bused in from the hills every day. Well, that does create a slight communication problem.

MICHELLE: I think I know what Kevin was attempting to say. He used two concepts; high visibility and geographical environment. Joe, let's just suppose that you lived in an all-black ghetto.

JOE: Suppose? My whole life has been one big ghetto experience. Believe me, I have not been beyond these walls; and I am serious about that.

MICHELLE: Well, if that's the case, surely you can understand the analogy that I am about to make. Again, you are living in an all-black ghetto, occasionally white people come into your community for one reason or another—when a white person comes into your community, he assumes high visibility. This simply means that the white person can be readily recognized because of the color of his skin. OK, when Africans were brought to America, the color of their skin made them highly visible among white and brown people. This made it extremely difficult for Africans to escape from slavery, because they could be recognized so easily.

JOE: I think I know what you mean, since you put it like that. But you still didn't explain what he meant about that other mile-long term that he used.

MICHELLE: Oh, you mean the "limited knowledge of the geographical environment"?

JOE: Yes, that's it.

MICHELLE: OK, I will try and explain what I think he meant. You see, the Indians had lived in Hispaniola for many years, and they were "hip" to their surroundings. That is, they knew all of the little trails, all of the big trails, all of the hideouts, all of the hide-ins. Brother, they knew their way around; and whenever they could no longer endure the hardships of the mines and the plantations, they hit the trails and to the hills they went. On the other hand, when the brothers were brought over from Africa, they didn't know anything about the little trails, the big trails, and the hideouts in the mountains. Therefore, the slave masters were able to exert more control over the Africans than they were over the Indians.

TEACHER: Very well said, Michelle. Surely all of the above reasons played a part in the enslavement of Africans in America. However, the most important factors would appear to be, first, the accessibility of Blacks in Africa, and the seemingly never-exhausted supply. Secondly, slave buyers were able to purchase African slaves at a very low price.

REGIE: Speaking of the seemingly never-exhausted supply of African slaves, approximately how many Africans were taken as slaves?

TEACHER: No one knows for certain. However, historians estimate that more than ten million Africans were taken into slavery before this most inhumane traffic could be brought to an end. If there are no additional questions or comments, let's move on to slavery in the colonies.

KEVIN: I have a question—a real burning question. How did Africans allow themselves to be taken into slavery in such great numbers. It appears to me that they didn't put forth any kind of united struggle. My question is—why?

TEACHER: You have to understand that Africans were greatly divided along tribal lines. Different tribes were constantly at war with each other; and when one tribe would conquer another tribe, they would usually enslave them. These tribal wars were increased greatly when the mines and plantations of America began to demand more and more slave labor.

KEVIN: I am not sure that I understand what you are saying.

TEACHER: I am only suggesting that African tribes engaged each other in war, and then sold their victims to European slave buyers, who in turn sold these slaves to mine and plantation owners in America.

LYNN: Are you really telling us that African tribal groups actually captured one another and sold them to white slave buyers.

TEACHER: It is true.

Discussion Questions

1. What were the encomiendas?
2. Give several reasons why the Indians didn't make good slaves?
3. Why were Blacks thought to be more desirable slaves than the Indians? Explain.
4. How did African tribal groups participate in the transatlantic slave trade?

5. What kind of work were the Indian men and women required to do?
6. Who was Bartolomé de Las Casas?

          Words you should know:

               tributes
               domestic
               plantation
               inhumane
               credible
               visibility
               environment
               revolt
               immunity
               antibody
               primary

Chapter 3

SLAVERY IN THE COLONIES

Persons of the Dialogue: Teacher, Regie, Tammie, Kevin, Tony, Lisa, Yogi, Angie, Lynn and Michelle.

... If these be chains—they are breakable ...

TEACHER: Slavery in the English Colonies, which later became the United States, developed in much the same manner as slavery developed in the West Indies.

REGIE: I am not sure that I understand what you are saying. Please, would you speak further.

TEACHER: Well, first of all, white plantation owners attempted to enslave the Indians as a cheap source of labor. However, as you will surely recall, the Indians didn't make good slaves in the West Indies, and for the same reason, they would not bear the chains of slavery in the English Colonies. However, when the Indians failed to serve the needs of the plantation owners, they then turned to indentured servants and European convicts.

TAMMIE: Who were the indentured servants and convicts? From whence did they come?

TEACHER: Mostly, they were white people from Europe, sent out under various forms of forced labor. Some of the convicts were taken from debtor's prison, while other had been convicted of felonies or very serious crimes. Anyway, these convicts were allowed to pay their debts to society by coming to America and working for a number of years.

TAMMIE: I am still not sure that I understand what is meant by indentured servants.

KEVIN: Perhaps I can explain it to you, Tammie. You see, there were many poor white people living in Europe. Many of these people wanted to make a better life for themselves and their families. They believed that they could do this if they could make it to the colonies in America. Therefore, these people agreed to work, usually four to seven years for anyone who would pay for their journey to America. After they had served their four to seven years, they were given their freedom.

TEACHER: You are quite correct, Kevin. However, we must hasten to add that the plantation owner's labor problem was not solved by the use of indentured servants.

TAMMIE: Why?

TEACHER: It appears that they wanted too much for too little.

TAMMIE: Meaning what?

TEACHER: The plantation owners wanted all of a man's productive years, and not just four to seven years of his life. As a result, they turned to a people who were most unlike them in culture, color, language, and background in general. Here again, just as in the West Indies, the burden of slavery fell upon the black man.

TONY: But isn't it true that the first Blacks who were brought to the Virginia colony served as indentured servants rather than slaves?

TEACHER: Yes, there appears to be sufficient evidence to suggest that those twenty Blacks who were brought and sold to the English colonists by the Dutch in 1619, served as indentured servants rather than slaves.

LISA: What evidence do you have to support the idea that the first Blacks, in the Virginia Colony, were indentured servants and not slaves?

TEACHER: OK, in 1624, John Phillips, one of the twenty Blacks brought to Jamestown, Virginia in 1619, by the Dutch, was a witness in a law suit.

LISA: That proves what?

TEACHER: It should prove that the first Blacks in the colony of Virginia were not slaves.

LISA: How did you arrive at that conclusion?

TEACHER: According to the English law which was in effect at that time, a slave had no legal status. He could not sue, be sued or bear witness in a court of law. Since John Phillips acted as a witness in a court of law—we, therefore, assume that he was not considered to be a slave.

LISA: Oh, I see.

YOGI: In addition to what the teacher just said, there are records which suggest that a child of one of the Black couples among the twenty Blacks at Jamestown, was later baptized a Christian. Again, according to English law in effect at the time, any person who was baptized was entitled to his freedom. I think that both of these cases support the notion that the first Blacks came as indentured servants and not as slaves.

ANGIE: If this was the case, why didn't all Blacks seek baptism so that they could gain their freedom?

TEACHER: Conversion to Christianity was one of the first steps sought by many as a means of acquiring their freedom. However, as we shall see later, conversion to Christianity, in spite of the English law, did not always mean freedom.

REGIE: Assuming that the first Blacks in the colonies were indentured servants, there seems to be little or no doubt that this status did not last long. As a matter of fact, as early as 1640, twenty years after the first Blacks arrived, one can hear the first mutterings of permanent slavery for Blacks.

TEACHER: How did you arrive at that conclusion?

REGIE: I read about the Manuel Case.

LYNN: What happened in the Manuel Case?

REGIE: Well, Manuel was a black man who had been purchased by a white man called Thomas Bushrod. Bushrod bought Manuel with the understanding that Manuel would be his slave forever. In 1644 the Assembly declared that Manuel was not a slave. However, the Assembly went on to say that Manuel had to remain with Bushrod for 21 years. This, of course, had gone a long, long way from the four to seven years that were usually required of indentured servants. In other words, it appears that by 1644, permanent slavery for Blacks was rapidly approaching.

TEACHER: Very well said, Regie.

KEVIN: There is another court case which took place in the early 1640s, and this case very definitely supports Regie's conclusion that permanent slavery was rapidly approaching for Blacks by the early 1640s.

TEACHER: What case are you speaking of now?

KEVIN: The Punch Case.

TONY: The Punch Case? Who got punched?

KEVIN: Be serious, Tony—this is no time to inject humor.

TONY: Sorry, I couldn't resist that one.

TEACHER: Now that we have had our bit of humor—Kevin, will you please proceed.

KEVIN: The Punch case involved three servants who tried to escape from their master. However, they were caught in the process of trying to escape. I think I should tell you that John Punch was a Black servant and the two men who tried to escape with him were white servants. After these men were caught trying to escape they were taken before a court of law. The court ruled that the two white men should serve their master for four additional years as a punishment for their behavior. What kind of punishment do you think Punch received?

TONY: The court probably said this is it for the rest of your days.

KEVIN: Did instinct or logic dictate that conclusion?

TONY: Oh, let's just assume that I have a kind of built-in radar for anticipating these kinds of things. After all, I have been Black for a long time.

KEVIN: But you are only fifteen years old, and you were not thought of during the historical period that we are discussing.

TONY: Have things really changed that much?

KEVIN: Well, I would surely hope so—I don't see any people walking around in chains today.

TONY: Well, then, what do you call those things that are restricting people to ghettos? Then, what do you call those things that are restricting people to barrios? You must surely understand, my friend, that chains come in many different forms and shapes; sometimes visible and sometimes invisible.

KEVIN: If these be chains—they are breakable!

TONY: You are right. However, in my short life, I have seen many people break their minds, bodies and spirits, before they were able to break the chains of poverty which form the boundaries of ghetto existence.

KEVIN: I guess you see things that I can't see.

TONY: Remember, Kevin, we are looking at this situation from a different point of view. I am on the inside trying to get out. Well as for you, your parents were able to escape, before the winds of poverty could blow your mind—for that, you should consider yourself very fortunate.

KEVIN: Perhaps I am fortunate. However, I could never be satisfied untill the walls of the ghetto come tumbling down for all of my people.

TONY: I only wish that more people shared your point of view.

ANGIE: I am sure that all of us share Kevin's point of view; however, I thought this was a history class and not a class on contemporary social problems.

KEVIN: It was never decreed that the two should not meet. However, if it pleases you, my dear little Angel, I shall gladly resume my little speech on John Punch and the court's decision.

TEACHER: I wish you would, Kevin; I think the class has been very patient while you and Tony exchanged you views on contemporary problems.

KEVIN: Well, there is much to be said about that; however, if you insist, I will talk about John Punch instead. As I said earlier, the two white men who attempted to escape with John Punch were given four additional years of servitude for their attempted escape. However, in the case of John Punch, the court said that he should serve his master for the rest of his life. Again, this should suggest that by the early 1640s, some courts were beginning to favor permanent slavery for Black people.

TEACHER: Before we discontinue our discussion of the early development of slavery in the colonies, there is one other case that I would like to call to your attention. This case involved a Black man and one of his Black servants.

MICHELLE: Black people had servants too?

TEACHER: It was rather rare—but some did. As a matter of record, Anthony Johnson, a former servant, gained his freedom and then he acquired large sums of land in Hampton County of Virginia. As his wealth increased he was able to secure the services of servants. However, in 1653, one of his servants, John Casor, who had served Johnson for 15 years, brought suit against him questioning the length of time that he was to serve. When the case went to court, Johnson claimed that Casor owed him service for life. I think it should be said that between the early 1640s and the late 1660s there was still a great deal of uncertainty as to whether Blacks should be classified as servants or permanent slaves. Finally, in 1662,

Virginia recognized the enslavement of Blacks as being both permanent and legal.

ANGIE: Earlier, it was said that the English law provided that persons who had been beptized would subsequently be given their freedom. If I have understood correctly, it appears that at the same time that more Blacks were becoming Christians, more of them were becoming slaves for life. Needless to say, I am very much confused.

TEACHER: Perhaps I can help you, Angie. In spite of the English law which suggested freedom for all baptized servants, from the early 1640s on, more Blacks were becoming permanent slaves, regardless of their religious beliefs. However, there was some concern about the legal and moral implications of enslaving a Christian. Therefore, in 1667, the Virginia legislature passed a law saying that the fact that a servant was baptized did not mean that he should be given his freedom.

MICHELLE: In other words, by the late 1660s, the road of escape for Black servants was almost closed. The signpost, held by slave masters, was increasingly saying—*no way out*.

TEACHER: Very well said, Michelle. I think I should add that as other colonies developed, they followed the pattern that had been set by Virginia. And by 1706, Maryland, North Carolina, New Jersey, South Carolina and New York had accepted the idea that baptism did not mean freedom for Black slaves. Once this religious problem had been solved, the enslavement of Blacks was a matter of how many do we need, how many can we get? Finally, as the demand for rice, indigo, and tobacco grew, so did the cries of many Africans—as they crossed the Atlantic, and took up the burden of slavery in the colonies.

Discussion Questions

1. What is an indentured servant?
2. Indentured servants did not solve the labor problems of the American plantation owners. Why? Explain.

3. The first Blacks brought to the English Colony of Virginia were not thought of as slaves. Why? Explain.
4. What was the Manuel case? How did this case affect the legal status of Black people?
5. What colony took the lead in making slavery permanent for Black people?

Words you should know:

colony
barrio
contemporary
legal
conversion
instinct
logic
historical
social

Chapter 4

GEOGRAPHY AND SLAVERY

Persons of the Dialogue: Teacher, Yogi, Sha, Jan, Regie, Kevin, Lisa, Tammie and Lynn.

> ... *As I see it, it is much better to try and understand it—than to pretend that it never happened* ...

TEACHER: Today we shall concern ourselves with the geographical implications of slavery in the colonies.

YOGI: Am I correct in saying that geography means the study of the earth and the way things are distributed on the earth?

TEACHER: I would say that's a very good definition of geography.

YOGI: In other words, we are going to be studying about the way in which slaves were distributed throughout the colonies.

TEACHER: Yes, I think it is important that we understand that some colonies were more dependent on slave labor than others. As a result, some colonies were more densely populated with slaves.

SHA: I am of the opinion that climate played a big part in the permanent enslavement of Blacks in the Southern colonies.

JAN: What do you mean, Sha? Are you suggesting that climate helps to determine how people think and behave toward each other? Ridiculous.

SHA: Perhaps not as ridiculous as you may think. Hear me out, and then we shall see if your mind remains in the very shallow realms of human affairs.

JAN: I am sure that I disagree with you; however, I was always taught to listen first and ask questions later, I guess I shouldn't treat you any differently. Speak.

SHA: Let me ask you a question—what do you consider the main reason for bringing Africans to the colonies in such great numbers?

JAN: Obviously, they needed cheap labor and they found it in the African slave trade.

SHA: Very well—what were most of the slaves used for?

JAN: In the early colonial period, most slaves were used in the tobacco, rice and indigo fields. However, in the early 1800s, more and more Blacks were used on cotton plantations.

SHA: Very well. Tell me, where did these crops grow?

JAN: You mean—what colonies?

SHA: Yes.

JAN: Well, if you must know, tobacco was grown on a very large scale in Virginia and North Carolina. Indigo and rice were grown in South Carolina and Georgia. Of course, in the early 1800s cotton plantations began to spread throughout the Southern colonies.

SHA: Now you have mentioned four colonies that demanded slaves on a very large scale during the early colonial period. Tell me, what did these colonies have in common?

JAN: All of them required lots of workers for their big plantations.

SHA: But that's to say the obvious. Is that all they had in common?

JAN: Well, no, not really. All of them were Southern co with very similar climates.

SHA: OK, in your opinion, did climate have anything to with the crops that were grown by the colonies.

JAN: Without a doubt; everyone knows that certain crops need special kinds of climates in which to grow. What are you getting at?

REGIE: Are you two going to monopolize the entire discussion —just maybe someone else has something to say.

SHA: I hope you will forgive me, because I am trying to make a point. Now, Jan, earlier you said that the big rice, tobacco and indigo plantations were located in the Southern colonies —right?

JAN: Right.

SHA: OK, If all of the big plantations were located in the South, was this a coincidence, or was there some specific reason for this?

JAN: Well, everyone knows that the Southern colonies had a much longer growing season; which was necessary for most of the crops that were grown on the big plantations.

SHA: OK, since the majority of the slaves lived in the South and worked on the plantations, it appears, to me, that climate had a great deal to do with developing and sustaining the slave system.

JAN: You seem very intent on proving your point; and by now I am willing to concede that your point is well made. However, let me remind you that slavery was also quite widespread throughout the Middle and New England colonies; and the climate was not conducive to the kind of plantation systems that developed in the South.

SHA: I didn't mean to suggest that climate was the only reason for the development of slavery in the colonies; however, it seems logical to assume that if large plantations had not developed in the South, slavery wouldn't have been nearly so desirable on such a large scale. I am really suggesting that the abolition of slavery met with far less resistance in the North than in the South, and in my opinion, climate played a big part in helping to keep slavery alive in the South.

TEACHER: Both of you have contributed greatly to the subject under discussion; however, let me say this in support of what has already been said. I think that historians would agree that soil and climate did not permit the extensive development of plantations in the North as it did in the South. At the same time, slavery was by no means insignificant in the economic development of the North. The North had a labor shortage problem just as the South did—and they, too, used slave labor to no small degree.

KEVIN: You said that the soil and the climate did not permit the extensive development of plantations in the North—my question is, what kind of work were slaves required to do in the North?

TEACHER: Slaves, in the North, were required to do many different jobs, including lumbering, mining, farming, printing, cabinetmaking, ropemaking and carpentry. Others worked in quarries, fisheries, tanneries, shipyards, laundries and factories. As you know, many worked as domestic servants. I might add that many of the above jobs required a great deal of skill.

LISA: Are you suggesting that many slaves were trained for skilled jobs?

TEACHER: Yes, indeed they were. However, the skill was not for the benefit of the slave, but for the master. The slave masters would often hire their slaves out, and any and all money earned by the slaves belonged to the slave masters. Occasionaly, some masters would give their slaves a small portion of the money they had earned; the rest of course they kept for themselves.

TAMMIE: That sure was cold.

KEVIN: You think that's cold—just wait until we talk about the way in which slaves were treated by their masters.

TAMMIE: You know, perhaps it would be better if we didn't talk about that. As a young Black person, I feel that I have enough historical insults to live with the rest of my life.

KEVIN: I think I know how you feel, Tammie. Two years ago when I first began to study Black history, I too felt a certain urge to let my past be buried in the archives of time. However, curiosity compelled me to read further; and as I read, I met some beautiful brothers and sisters who challenged me to walk where they had walked—at least in spirit.

TAMMIE: Are you challenging me?

KEVIN: I am commanding you. I am of the opinion that no black person can be free in spirit or in deed until he has walked in the path of his ancestors.

TAMMIE: I am not sure that I get your meaning—would you please speak further?

KEVIN: You see, Tammie, and this certainly applies to all of us, the height of a people may never be reached if they are cut off from their history. This fact was well known by slaves masters, and they tried by every trick that they knew to deny Afro-Americans a knowledge of their heritage.

TAMMIE: I see—I think I know what you mean. You seem so well informed, perhaps you could recommend some books that I should read. But, remember, you must be very selective in your recommendations, because I don't wish to have my spirit shaken by the inhumane behavior of little-minded slave drivers. I have enough burdens to bear.

KEVIN: I am afraid that would not be possible or desirable. I need not remind you that the history of Afro-Americans is long and filled with disappointments and hardships—the kind that have subjected Black people to the most difficult kind of human struggle. Those of us who would seek to know more about ourselves must by necessity seek to better understand our history. However bitter the past may have been, you too, must taste of it.

TAMMIE: You make it sound like a very urgent matter.

KEVIN: I was never more serious.

TAMMIE: If indeed I must journey into the distant years of the Black experience, I will surely need someone to guide and comfort me, because my vision is not clear; and the values of the Western world have slightly confused me.

KEVIN: Very well, my sister, I should be glad to recommend someone to guide you through the winding roads of the Black experience in America. Do you prefer a male or a female?

TAMMIE: Preferably a female—I think it is high time that women take their rightful place in the history of mankind.

KEVIN: I can very well relate to what you are saying; and I am pleased to recommend two of America's most outstanding women, Sojourner Truth and Harriet Tubman. Both have unquestionable credentials, and either would make an excellent guide. Believe me, they know the way and their scars will surely attest to that.

LISA: You didn't mention Phillis Wheatley; I wonder why—did you forget?

KEVIN: No, I didn't forget, and I am sure that most of us can agree that Phillis was a beautiful sister—her poetry was surely alive. However, she bears no scars, and she may not know the way. Her situation was surely unique among Black people of her time.

LISA: You know something, Kevin, you make it sound as if these people are still alive.

KEVIN: Yes, Lisa, I think they are very much alive. You know, I learned quite early in my life that good deeds and well-spoken ideas never die—they have a way of commanding the attention of one generation after another.

YOGI: You said that Phillis Wheatley may not know the way because she bears no scars. I am not sure that I understand that—would you please elaborate on that statement?

KEVIN: Well, according to history, Phillis Wheatley arrived in Boston Harbor, in chains, in the year of 1761. Phillis was approximately eight years old at the time of her arrival. Like other Blacks arriving from Africa, she had no idea as to what this strange land held for her. However, as fate would have it, she was purchased by a wealthy, white family in Boston. It is said that they accepted Phillis as one of the family. She was educated and exposed to the better things in life. She was indeed one of the few Africans who had the opportunity to develop their minds and talents. Phillis was considered by many as one of the truly outstanding poets of her time. Most of all, she was spared the lashes and inhumane treatments of cruel slave masters. This is why I said she may not know the way; her experience was radically different from most Blacks of her time.

YOGI: Indeed it was.

LYNN: Were slaves really treated as badly as we have been led to believe?

TEACHER: Yes, the plight of slaves was very dismal. Some may have been treated better than others—but in general, slaves were treated as personal property—like a mule or a cow. As a means of controlling slaves, Southern colonies passed very rigid slave codes or laws. If the slaves didn't obey these codes, they were whipped, branded and sometimes put to death. Of course there were other forms of punishment that were so gruesome that I would rather not speak of them here. However, in subsequent dialogue, we shall speak once again of the cruel and unusual punishments imposed upon those Blacks who attempted to resist the yoke of slavery.

TAMMIE: I am glad that you made the decision not to speak further about the punishments of slaves. As you know, the subject is a very sensitive one, and personally, I can't digest too much at one time.

TEACHER: I thought you would say that, Tammie; and I am sure there are others who feel the same way. However, before we discontinue our discussion, I would like for someone to briefly summarize the main ideas that have claimed our attention for the past thirty minutes.

SHA: I think it should be said that the majority of the slaves lived in the South and worked on large plantations. It appears that *climate* had a great deal to do with the fact that slavery lived so long in the South, and destroyed the lives of so many. However, as Jan pointed out earlier, slavery was by no means insignificant in the development of Northern colonies. But it appears that the soil and climate discouraged the extensive development of plantations in the North, and as a result, the demand for slave labor was far less than it was in the South. However, I continue to arrive at the conclusion that *geography* played a big part in the permanent enslavement of Black people.

KEVIN: Historians and social critics will probably debate the causes and the effects of slavery for many years to come. However, the conclusion that they reach will certainly not alter the fact that slavery was a most traumatic experience for those black people who had to endure it. It was indeed an experience that many of us would rather forget, but for some strange reason, the effects of it all keep coming up, again and again, and as we shall see, *again*. However, as I see it, it is much better to try and understand it—than to pretend that it never happened. In other words, brothers and sisters, as we better understand the past, we shall be better prepared to cope with the present and the future. I am really trying to say that a good knowledge of history is a very important part of our education.

TEACHER: I was going to say more, however, I think Kevin has said it better than I could say it. Therefore, I urge you to give his statement some serious thought before you write off history as being irrelevant to your present situation. Because, as Kevin has said, the effects of it all will surely come up, again, again, and perhaps again.

Discussion Questions

1. Why were some colonies more dependent on slave labor than others?

2. Before the 1800s, what were the main crops grown in Southern colonies?
3. Give several ways in which slaves were used in Northern colonies.
4. What is meant by the statement, "Phillis Wheatley may not know the way because she bears no scars."
5. Did climate and soil play a big part in the development of the plantation system in the South? Explain.

Words you should know:

geography
indigo
climate
monopolize
concede
heritage
generation
subsequent

Chapter 5

DID SLAVES DARE REVOLT?

Persons of the Dialogue: Teacher, Yogi, Angie, Michelle, Bob, Joe, Tony, Darryl and Joseph.

... You mean they had "Toms" in those days ...

TEACHER: Some historians have suggested that slaves were complacent, satisfied, and happy with their situations as servants. A few weeks a go, some of you undertook this subject as a research project. I think you have had adequate time to do your research and prepare your findings. Therefore, if all of you are ready, I suggest that we begin our discussion.

YOGI: Well, as far as I am concerned, this whole thing is just another myth.

TEACHER: On what grounds do you draw your conclusions?

YOGI: On the grounds that there is too much documented evidence to the contrary. However, this is not to suggest that slaves didn't make some adjustments to the very inhumane situation that they found themselves in; obviously, if slaves had not made adjustments, survival would have been next to impossible. According to my research, slavery was met with varied degrees and kinds of resistance from the beginning of the transatlantic slave trade in the early 1500s to the end of chattel slavery in the late 1800s.

TEACHER: If resistance was as common as you say, what from did this resistance take? By that I mean, how did the slaves make their masters know that they were not pleased with their situations?

ANGIE: I would like to speak to that question. There were many ways in which slaves resisted the demands of their masters. For example, on the Sea Islands along the coast of South Carolina, slaves from the Ebo Tribe of Africa committed suicide in great numbers. Many of them simply walked into the water and drowned themselves, rather than submit to the chains of slavery. I might add that some parents killed their own children rather than have them become slaves.

MICHELLE: Killed their own children—a bitter choice to make for sure. But in the final analysis, I would say that no one, including parents, has the right to make that decision for another person.

ANGIE: I agree with you; however, under those circumstances, I would imagine that one does not think of rights—but only choices. And to be a slave was more than some parents could endure for their children, as well as themselves.

BOB: Another very common means of resisting slavery was the destruction of property. For example some slaves would abuse the livestock, while others would intentionally destroy the farm equipment. The destruction of property by fire was particularly disturbing to the slave masters. On many occasions, slave masters saw their barns, filled with tobacco and grain, go up in flames. If a slave was caught in this kind of act, he was usually put to death. In spite of this, many took their chances.

YOGI: If I may add to what has already been said, another form of slave resistance was the faking of illness. This, apparently, was a very common form of resistance. Some historians suggest that when there were difficult tasks to be done on the plantations, illness among slaves greatly increased, and as Sunday approached, illness usually decreased noticeably.

JOE: It appears evident that slaves used every trick that they could contrive to try to beat the slave master at his game. Obviously, they were not always successful.

ANGIE: There is yet another form of slave resistance that has not been mentioned.

TONY: What is that?

ANGIE: Flight.

TONY: Meaning what?

ANGIE: Meaning they simply ran away. Some slaves ran away alone, while others joined up with organized groups and escaped by way of the Underground Railroad.

DARRYL: Maybe I am naive, but be that as it may—did they really have underground railroads in those days—you know, with trains taking slaves to the North?

TEACHER: No, Darryl, the Underground Railroad was a system set up for the purpose of helping runaway slaves escape to the North.

DARRYL: But was it a train?

TEACHER: It was a train of people, both black and white, working together for the purpose of helping slaves escape from their masters. In order to do this, they had to make sure that their activities were carried out in the greatest of secrecy. This organization, however, did not come into existence untill the 1800s.

DARRYL: I see.

TEACHER: There is yet another very important form of slave resistance which we have not discussed at all.

YOGI: I was just going to say that we have not discussed insurrections and revolts.

TEACHER: This is precisely what I had in mind. Who will lead us?

YOGI: Well, there are probably many small-scale revolts and insurrections which never got into the history books. However, there is evidence to suggest that as early as 1712, a rather serious revolt took place in New York City. According to my research, this revolt involved some twenty-three slaves who rose up against their masters. As a result of this revolt, nine whites were killed.

ANGIE: What happened to those poor defenseless slaves?

YOGI: Just as you might imagine, they met with death in a very terrifying manner. Some were burned, others hanged, but all met their final destiny in a most barbaric fashion. However, the quest for freedom is a powerful thing, and as we shall see, slave revolts kept on coming, in spite of the consequences.

MICHELLE: Apparently there were more slave uprisings in some colonies than others. My research indicates that between 1720 and 1740 South Carolina witnessed many slave revolts; and some of them, such as the Stono Uprising in 1739, caused great alarm and panic among white people throughout the Southeast.

JOSEPH: What happened in the Stono Case?

MICHELLE: According to my research, about twenty Black brothers from Angola got their heads together, and under the direction of their leader, Tommy, they begin marching and beating drums attempting to encourage other to join them. When the revolt was finally over, several whites were killed and a great deal of property had been destroyed.

JOSEPH: Well, I guess I don't need to ask what happened to these brothers after the uprising—but, I'll ask anyway.

MICHELLE: You know, I must say, the brothers did a very strange thing; perhaps this was in keeping with their African customs. However, when the revolt was over, they marched to a nearby field and began to sing and dance. It was here that the militia came upon them and engaged them in a great and bloody battle. As you might suspect, the African brothers lost the battle, as well as their lives, but they fought to the end for their freedom.

TEACHER: Obviously, we will not be able to discuss all of the revolts and would-be revolts; however, there were some very serious revolts that we have not yet talked about.

JOSEPH: What do you mean by "would-be revolts"?

TEACHER: According to history, many of the slave plots were aborted or failed to develop beyond the planning stage. Very often, many of the plans to revolt did not develop because someone, usually another slave, would inform the master.

JOSEPH: You mean they had "Toms" in those days?

TEACHER: I am not sure that I know what you mean by *Tom,* but if a "Tom" is the same as an informer—well, they have been around a long, long time.

JOSEPH: You understood my meaning very well—but I was just sitting here thinking. You know that was very cold for one brother to "Tom," or as you say, inform on the other brothers. Now I see why it took the brothers so long to gain their freedom.

TEACHER: As you shall see, Joseph, that was only a very small part of the slave's inability to gain his freedom.

JOSEPH: Yes, I am sure there were mountains much taller than the brothers called "Toms."

TEACHER: Before we talk about revolts and uprisings in the United States during the early 1800s—perhaps we should talk about a slave uprising that took place in the West Indies during the 1790s.

TONY: Teacher, you call that an uprising—that was a full-scale war. Those brothers got their heads together, and Haiti went up in smoke.

MICHELLE: Haiti is in the West Indies—right?

TEACHER: Yes.

MICHELLE: Sometime ago, I remember reading about the Haitian slave revolt—but at this point, I can't really recall what happened.

TONY: According to my research, in 1791, the Haitian slaves petitioned the French National Assembly for their freedom. When they were denied their freedom by the Assembly, they then decided that the only way that they could gain their freedom was to take it.

DARRYL: Did they take it?

TONY: Hear me out and then judge for yourself. On August 14, 1791, the Haitian sky became a ball of fire. Sugar mills burned, cornfields burned, houses burned, and whole plantations burned.

DARRYL: Hey, Tony—are you sure you are not describing the 1965 Watts Rebellion?

TONY: We'll get to Watts later, and we might even call it Haiti Revisited. But for now, let's concentrate on Haiti in the 1790s. At the beginning of the revolt, only the slaves were fighting against the Haitian whites. However, as the fighting went on, the free blacks and the mulattos realized that they too, had a cause; so they joined up with the slaves and soon this all-Black army had swelled to some one hundred thousand strong. A mighty force, in quest of that precious thing called freedom.

ANGIE: Is this the same revolt that saw that little ugly man become such a great leader? I don't remember his name, but as a student of wars and revolutions, I am sure you recognize the description.

TONY: I presume you are talking about the great Toussaint l'Ouverture.

ANGIE: Yes, that's his name.

TONY: Toussaint had so many excellent qualities that I am sure you could have been more positive in your description of him. However, I am aware that history speaks of him as not being the most handsome of men—nevertheless, the brilliance of his mind surely compensates for any lack of physical appearance.

YOGI: In addition to what Tony just said, I might add that Toussaint was not a member of the group which started the revolt. He didn't join the revolt until about a month after it began. And as we shall see, he became one of the most brilliant leaders of all times.

DARRYL: Did Toussaint grow up as a slave?

TONY: Yes, he grew up as a slave.

DARRYL: Well, how do you account for the fact that he was able to develop his intelligence to such a high level, and then become such a great military leader?

TONY: Well, this can probably be attributed to the fact that his master thought very highly of him, and encouraged him to read about history, politics, economics, and especially military science. In addition, Toussaint's master made him head coachman and overseer of all the livestock on the plantation. These jobs were usually held by white men.

TEACHER: We have been talking in general about the leadership abilities of Toussaint—perhaps we could be a little more specific and talk about some of his accomplishments as a military leader. In other words, what did he do as a military leader that has caused historians to speak of him as an outstanding personality in Haitian history?

TONY: Well, first of all, he brought very highly developed military skills to the revolutionary movement. Secondly, he gave organization to the movement, and set up military training programs which would later test the military strength of both French and British forces.

MICHELLE: If Haiti was a French colony, what were the British doing there?

TONY: Well, you see, French Haiti was a very rich and prosperous colony. As a result, a number of European nations were very much interested in Haiti. In addition, Britain and France were already at war in Europe; therefore, since France was having problems with the colony in Haiti, Britain thought this was a good time to come in and try to take over. However, the British were finally driven out of Haiti by the military forces of Toussaint in 1798.

DARRYL: It appears that Toussaint was a powerful Black brother.

MICHELLE: And that's for sure.

TONY: There is much more to come. By 1801, things had calmed down in Haiti, and Toussaint was very much in control. He had gained the support and confidence of mulattos, Blacks and whites. At last, he was recognized as the governor general of all of Haiti.

MICHELLE: Tell me, Tony, how do you know so much about Toussaint and the Haitian Revolution?

TONY: Well, when I was still in elementary school, my father began telling me about Toussaint and his struggle against the forces of slavery. As I grew older, my curiosity compelled me to increase my knowledge of this man, and I am glad that I did. He was one of the most interesting individuals that I have had the opportunity to read about.

TEACHER: After the revolution was over in 1801, Haiti was obviously in a state of social, political and economic confusion. Hundreds of plantations had been destroyed, thousands of people had lost their lives, including both Blacks and whites. However, within eighteen months, two-thirds of the land that had been used under the old system, was ready for cultivation again. I ask you, how did Toussaint accomplish so much in such a short period of time. How did he do it?

TONY: Well, the first thing he did was to divide the island up into six provinces. He then revised the finance and tax laws, built schools, created courts of law, and encouraged plantation owners to return to their plantations so that the economy could be rebuilt. In addition, he wrote a new constitution for

Haiti. In this constitution, Toussaint was named governor for life; he was also given the power to name the man who should be his successor.

ANGIE: A truly amazing brother—he really had a lot going for himself.

TONY: Indeed he did, until one day he looked around and Napoleon's army was looking over his shoulder.

DARRYL: What did they want?

TONY: They wanted to get rid of Brother Toussaint, and return all Black people to the chains of slavery. In order to do this, Napoleon sent General Leclerc and 23,000 troops to Haiti.

DARRYL: I can imagine that they were entertained sufficiently.

TONY: Well, I can assure you that they didn't really catch him holding his hands. As a matter of fact, you might say that he was expecting them. This is evidenced by the fact that he had given all of his able-bodied men military training.

JOE: In other words, the brother had put it all together before Napoleon's troops arrived.

TONY: Let's just say that the Black brothers of Haiti had tasted the sweetness of freedom, and they were not about to give it back to Napoleon or any other foreign power. However, apparently Napoleon was not aware of the deep convictions that these brothers held in regards to their freedom—so he pressed, and the forces of their military power met head-on. And blood flowed throughout the land.

ANGIE: You mean to say that Toussaint's army stood up against the mighty Napoleon of France?

TONY: It is written. I think one could truthfully say that Napoleon met his "Waterloo" in Haiti, before he was finally defeated at Waterloo in Europe.

MICHELLE: What was the final act?

TONY: When Napoleon's general, Leclerc, was unable to destroy Toussaint's army by force, he then began to bargain with Toussaint's top generals and persuaded them to join up with the French army. This greatly weakened Toussaint's military position and, as a result, he decided to retire. Fearful of Toussaint's presence in Haiti, Leclerc had him captured and sent to France. Upon his arrival in France, Napoleon ordered him into a mountain dungeon to await his final end.

TEACHER: On April 7, 1803, in a dark French dungeon, Toussaint came to the end of a journey—a journey which had seen him raise the banner of freedom throughout the land of Haiti. His pursuit of freedom had echoed around the world, and slaves everywhere were encouraged by his heroic deeds. He met his end, but the cause for which he had fought was not to be denied. Seven months after his death, Napoleon was finally convinced that Haitian Blacks could not be forced back into the chains of slavery.

TONY: After Napoleon had spilled the blood of some 60,000 French soldiers and sailors, he finally realized that the taste of freedom is a most powerful thing. As a matter of fact, too powerful to be put down by military might.

Discussion Questions

1. Give several ways in which slaves attempted to resist the chains of slavery?
2. What was the Underground Railroad?
3. Briefly describe the Haitian revolt or revolution. Why did it take place?
4. In your opinion, was Toussaint l'Ouverture a great leader? Why? or why not?
5. What is meant by the statement, "The taste of freedom is a powerful thing."
6. Where are the Sea Islands located?

Words you should know:

complacent
research

chattel
contrive
insurrection
destiny
rebellion
compensate
military
revolution
constitution

Chapter 6

SLAVE REVOLTS IN THE 1800s

Persons of the Dialogue: Teacher, Teddy, Joseph, Lisa, Yogi, Darryl, Joe, Angie, Michelle, Derric, Tony, and Regie.

> ... *The quest of freedom is a powerful thing; and a most dangerous thing for those who stand in the way* ...

TEACHER: In the past dialogue, we talked primarily about revolts and revolutions that took place in the 1700s. In addition, we were particularly concerned about the Haitian Revolution and the accomplishments of Toussaint l'Ouverture. It is important that we understand that, not only did the Haitian Revolution have far-reaching consequences for the slaves of Haiti, but at the same time, it greatly heightened the desire for freedom among slaves in the United States.

TEDDY: In what way?

TEACHER: Who would like to comment on that question?

JOSEPH: I would like to give my unbiased opinion.

TEACHER: If that is possible, proceed.

JOSEPH: As you will surely recall from the previous dialogue, in 1791, the Haitian slaves revolted in pursuit of their freedom. By 1800, slaves in the United States were well aware of what was going on in Haiti. As a result of the Haitian struggle, slaves in the United States were encouraged to become more active in the pursuit of their freedom.

LISA: You said that slaves in the United States were greatly encouraged by the efforts of slaves in Haiti. Does this mean that slaves in the United States were encouraged to try, as a group, to do something about their situation?

JOSEPH: Yes, I believe history certainly points in that direction. As a matter of record, in 1800, while the slaves in Haiti were yet fighting for their freedom, a slave, Gabriel Prosser of Virginia, was organizing a similar uprising. It is estimated that Prosser's plot may have involved more than 2000 slaves.

TEDDY: What were their plans, and how successful were they in implementing those plans?

JOSEPH: According to my research, their immediate plans were to take over an arsenal and several other important buildings in Richmond, Virginia. At this point they were to attack their white oppressors. If they were successful, it was thought that thousands of additional slaves would join them. Beyond this stage of planning, we know very little.

YOGI: Judging from what you just said, I would presume that the revolt never took place.

TEACHER: As a matter of fact, the planned revolt didn't take place. Does anyone know why?

LISA: As I understand it, after they had completed their plans, they had to travel about six miles to Richmond, where they were to launch their first attack. However, before they arrived in Richmond, a heavy rainstorm came and flooded the roads and bridges, making it impossible to go forward to Richmond as scheduled.

DARRYL: But there is another very important reason that the brothers didn't launch their attack as planned.

JOE: What was the other reason?

DARRYL: The "Toms" put the mouth on them.

LISA: Meaning what?

DARRYL: Meaning there were some poor Black brothers who thought they could make their burdens a little lighter if they told the white people what the Blacks were attempting to do. It is said that two Black brothers informed the whites of the Blacks' planned attack on Richmond, Virginia. Therefore, as a result, the governor called out more than six thousand troops and many arrests were made. For their part in the planned attack, thirty-five Blacks were hanged, including the leader, Gabriel Prosser.

YOGI: A real tragedy.

DARRYL: Has it been any other way?

YOGI: You know, in spite of the fact that this plot didn't develop beyond the planning stage, there is still something very incredible about this whole thing.

DARRYL: To what do you refer?

YOGI: I refer to the fact that hundreds of people were involved in this planned attack; and yet, the slave masters only learned about it a few days before it was to take place. It is all the more unbelievable, when you consider that the plot was in the making for such a long period of time, and whites were not aware of what was going on. This kind of planning must have taken excellent leadership and organization.

JOE: In my opinion, this kind of organized effort on the part of slaves would tend to put down the theory advanced by many traditional historians, who have suggested that slaves were happy, content and satisfied with their situation as slaves. The more I read, the more I am convinced that the facts don't always fit their conclusions.

TEACHER: It is indeed difficult to imagine an uprising of this size developing without the plantation owners having knowledge of it. However, it might help you to know that most of the planning took place at religious meetings. During these religious meetings, Gabriel Prosser and his brother, Martin, often shared the biblical experiences of the Israelites with their congregations. They assured their followers that, just as God had delivered the children of Isreal out of the hands of the Egyptians, he would deliver them from the hands of their oppressors.

ANGIE: In other words, Prosser and his followers were responding to a religious call, as well as the slave revolt that was taking place in Haiti. If this is true, one may conclude that religion didn't always lull slaves to sleep, and cause them to be more receptive to slavery, as some contemporary thinkers would lead us to believe.

TEACHER: Very well. I can assure you that all slaves did not always accept Saint Paul's mandate, "Servants, be obedient to your masters." Instead, many pointed to the Israelites' throwing off the yoke of bondage in Egypt and moving on the land of freedom. This idea was very prevalent among slave leaders of the late eighteenth and early nineteenth centuries.

JOE: Did they attempt to punish all of those slaves that were involved in the Prosser uprising?

TEACHER: No, that would have been impossible; there were too many people involved. However, as we have already suggested, they hanged Gabriel Prosser and thirty-four other slaves who were thought to be leaders. Of course, the mere fact that one was a slave—that in itself was a severe punishment.

JOE: It is encouraging to know that in spite of cruel and inhumane punishments received by Prosser and thirty-four other brothers, as we shall see, the quest for freedom continued.

TEACHER: In a few short sentences, how would anyone of you describe Gabriel Prosser?

MICHELLE: First of all, Gabriel Prosser was a man. Secondly, he was a Black religious man who had lofty plans of gaining the freedom of his people. As fate would have it, he was not able to carry out those plans. However, I think it should be said that, in spite of his religious beliefs, he was not willing to sacrifice his life, and his people's lives for a piece of pie in the sky, which was promised by money-loving plantation owners. Instead, he demanded a share of the fruits of this earth—of course, it cost him his life, but he did it his way.

TEACHER: Joe, suppose you were asked to write an epitaph for Gabriel Prosser, what would you write?

JOE: After giving it some serious thought, I suppose I would say: Here lies a friend of freedom. When the bells tolled for human freedom, he stood up and claimed it for himself and his people—a great and noble deed.

TEACHER: As we have already seen, the punishments for inciting slave revolts were indeed severe. However, in spite of the severity of the punishments, they kept on coming. It appears that many slaves were of the opinion that nothing could be worse than spending a lifetime in chains.

ANGIE: Just as you said, they kept on coming, and unfortunately, they kept on dying for the cause of freedom. As a matter or fact, some twenty years after Prosser's attempted revolt in Virginia, the scene changes to South Carolina. Here, Telemanque, known in history as Denmark Vesey, attempted to lead a slave revolt similar to the one led by Prosser.

DERRIC: Yes, I remember reading about him. He was a Methodist minister and he often held meetings in his house.

YOGI: Religious meetings?

DERRIC: Well, the plantation owners thought they were religious meetings. However, there is sufficient evidence to suggest that they were not spending all of their time, singing, shouting and praying. As a matter of fact, at least some of their time was spent planning a slave revolt, which was in the making for some two years.

YOGI: This sounds like another very well-organized plot.

DERRIC: Well, you see, Denmark Vesey was one of the few slaves who learned to read and write. In addition, he learned a great deal about business, because he was a constant companion of his master. As a matter of fact, after he purchased his freedom for $600, he became a very successful businessman.

MICHELLE: Are you suggesting that Vesey was not a slave when he was planning the slave uprising?

DERRIC: No, by this time, he had purchased his freedom. However, he was not content with freedom just for himself; but more than anything else, he wanted freedom for all slaves.

MICHELLE: How did he go about organizing the people over such a long period of time, and at the same time, keep it a secret.

DERRIC: As I said earlier, Denmark Vesey became a minister, and he used his home as a meeting place. I also said earlier that religious matters were not always the most important things discussed at their meetings. There is evidence to suggest that they spent much of their time preparing for a slave revolt. They collected money to buy weapons. They employed a blacksmith to make large supplies of daggers and bayonets. Also, plans were made to have mulattos disguise themselves as whites and move into the city and take over on the day of the attack.

TONY: Oh, I see, during slavery, Blacks often used religious meetings as a front to conceal their real activities.

DARRYL: Well, brother, they really had no other choice. This was the only way slave masters would allow Blacks to assemble in rather large numbers. Therefore, they tried to make the most of it; a little praying, a little preaching and a little planning.

ANGIE: After two years of planning, were Vesey and his followers successful in putting their plans into action?

DARRYL: No, I am afraid they weren't. Once again, a few days before the revolt was to take place, a Black brother whom Vesey had trusted revealed the plans to the slave master. Of course, this was the end of the planned revolt, as well as the end for Denmark Vesey and thirty-four other slaves. They all met their end in the usual way—hanging from the gallows.

TEACHER: In view of what has been said, how do you think history should remember Vesey?

MICHELLE: I believe history should say of him: He was a brave man, who found the courage to lead his people in the struggle against the evils of their time. He was not successful in executing his plan, however, he was very successful in that he reaffirmed the fact that Blacks would not accept slavery as a way of life.

TEACHER: Darryl, suppose you were charged with the responsibility of writing Vesey's epitaph—what would it be?

DARRYL: Though I die a thousand deaths—let my people go.

TEACHER: Very well said. This concludes our discussion of revolts, insurrections and revolutions.

REGIE: Did you forget, or would you rather not remember?

TEACHER: Remember what, Regie?

REGIE: Nat Turner.

TEACHER: How could I forget?

REGIE: Apparently you did. You led us to believe that we had concluded our discussion on revolts.

TEACHER: Maybe I was just testing to see if anyone would recall.

REGIE: Or, maybe you were afraid that we might ask you to write Nat's epitaph.

TEACHER: To that charge, I will surely answer. But for now let's go to Southampton County, Virginia, in August of 1831. Who will lead us?

REGIE: I'll try. The third major slave uprising in the early nineteenth century was led by a slave, Nat Turner. It is said that Nat Turner was a very strange man. He dreamt dreams, he saw visions, and most of all, he was sure that God had charged him with the responsibility of leading his Black sisters and brothers to freedom.

MICHELLE: In addition to what you said, Regie, it appears that Nat Turner made a lasting impression on most people who met him when he was still a very young child. According to history, Nat was an extremely bright young child, he was thought to be much more intelligent than the average child his age. Furthermore, there were birthmarks, which, according to African custom, indicated that Nat was born for some great purpose.

REGIE: Another note or interest on the life of Nat Turner suggests that when he was still a very young boy, his father escaped from the slave plantation and never returned. As Nat grew older, he thought of doing the same thing. As a matter of fact, he once ran away and spent thirty days in the wilderness, but after thinking it over, he returned to the plantation.

LISA: Was Nat Turner a preacher? I have always heard that he was.

REGIE: Yes, when he was about twenty-five years old, he began to think of himself as a preacher, and he often preached to the slaves. Nat learned how to read and write when he was a small child, and as a result, he could read the Bible very well and often quoted the Bible to support his stand against the evils of slavery.

LISA: A few minutes ago, you said that Nat Turner once ran away, and spent thirty days in the wilderness, but then he returned. Why did he return, after being gone for such a long time?

REGIE: As I said earlier, Nat was convinced that God had chosen him to lead the slaves to freedom. If he had escaped alone, he wouldn't have been helping his brothers and sisters who were still chained to Southern plantations. Again, he felt responsible for freeing all of the slaves—not just himself. Therefore, he returned to the plantation and took up the sword.

LISA: What then?

REGIE: He gathered his little band of slave brothers, and six of them went into the woods. There, these six men planned a slave revolt that shook the chains of slaves throughout the South. White people all over the South stood in fear and trembling—many state and federal troops were called out to deal with Nat Turner and his followers.

LISA: But you didn't tell us what Nat Turner and his followers did.

REGIE: Well, when they had finished making their plans there in the woods, they then moved swiftly upon Nat's master and the four members of his family. After taking their lives, they marched on, gathering arms and urging other slaves to join them. Their mission, of course, was to kill all slaveholders and their families. This however, was not accomplished, but, before Nat Turner and his followers could be stopped, ten men, fourteen women, and thirty-five white children lay dead.

LISA: You know it is difficult to believe that Nat Turner would do this kind of thing—because during his early years, he was thought of as being a very peaceful man who didn't believe in violence.

REGIE: I think that proves what we have been saying all the time. That is, the quest of freedom is a powerful thing; and a most dangerous thing for those who stand in the way.

LISA: Isn't it unfortunate that human beings have to resort to violence in order to make others recognize their right to "life, liberty, and the pursuit of happiness."

REGIE: I agree with you. However, looking back, one can see that the pages of history are replete with the blood of those who denied others the right to choose their own destiny.

TEACHER: Obviously, there are many slave conspiracies and revolts that we have not mentioned. As a matter of fact, some historians have recorded more than 200 slave conspiracies and revolts. Therefore, I would hope that some of you would be inspired to further pursue the study of slave resistance. Perhaps some of you can help to rewrite the pages of history.

REGIE: Teacher, before we conclude our dialogue on slave resistance, it just occured to me that you didn't ask anyone to say a final word, or write an epitaph for Nat Turner. I wonder why?

TEACHER: Young man, I have lived a few years longer than all of you; and time and circumstances have taught me that some people deliver their own eulogies, and write their own epitaphs, while struggling against the forces of nature, and the injustices of men. As for Nat Turner, he wrote his own, and neither history nor time can undo it. We can only hope that men would learn from these kinds of experiences. However, as we shall see, thousands of men died on the battlefield in the Civil War before Southern plantation owners would deal with the message that Nat Turner had attempted to deliver some thirty years earlier. Well, I guess men don't learn easily.

Discussion Questions

1. How did the slave uprising in Haiti affect the slaves in the United States?
2. What were Gabriel Prosser's plans? Was he successful in carrying out his plans? Explain.
3. Describe Denmark Vesey's attempt to lead the slaves in a revolt? What was the outcome of this attempt?
4. What kind of person was Nat Turner? How did he attempt to free the slaves?

Words you should know:

traditional
mulatto
conceal

epitaph
custom
replete
resistance
eulogy

Chapter 7

ABOLITIONISTS—PART I

Persons of the Dialogue: Teacher, Sha, Jan, Kevin, Derric and Teddy.

> ... *Are you suggesting that it is better to die young for a good cause, than to live into old age without a cause ...*

TEACHER: Nat Turner's revolt was the last major slave revolt of the nineteenth century. The repercussions of this revolt were heard resounding throughout America. Some historians feel that this revolt accelerated the coming of the abolitionist movement.

SHA: What was the abolitionist movement?

TEACHER: It was a movement started in the early 1830s. Its purpose was to bring an end to slavery. I might add that both Blacks and whites were involved in this movement.

JAN: Are you suggesting that there were white people who were concerned about the freedom of slaves?

TEACHER: Yes, this was true of many whites in the North; and some Southern whites agitated against slavery. Of course, you know that most Southern whites did not own any slaves.

KEVIN: Yes that's true. However, one must not interpret that to mean that most of the Southern whites were against slavery. The fact of the matter is that most Southern whites could not afford to own slaves. After all, slaves were expensive.

TEACHER: Your point is well made, and I am inclined to agree with you. However, before we get into further discussion of the abolitionist movement of the 1830s, I think we should mention the name David Walker.

KEVIN: Yes indeed, he was a heavy brother.

TEACHER: Then you know of him?

KEVIN: Yes, after digging deep into the archives of the library, I discovered him.

SHA: He must have impressed you.

KEVIN: Very deeply.

SHA: What was he about?

KEVIN: Much more than I can say here. However, as I recall, it was in 1829, two years before Nat Turner's revolt, he wrote a deep and moving analysis of the slave's situation. This analysis was called the "Appeals."

DERRIC: The Appeals?

KEVIN: Yes, it was called the Appeals. In these articles, Walker was attempting to touch the moral conscience of white America, and particularly the slaveholders.

DERRIC: Was he successful in this very lofty endeavor?

KEVIN: Unfortunately, he was not successful in achieving what he had hoped to achieve. If he had been successful to the extent that he desired, Nat Turner's revolt would not have been necessary, and neither would the Civil War.

JAN: Kevin, you appear to be very knowledgeable or the accomplishments of David Walker—would you speak more about him, I should like to know him better.

KEVIN: Well any man with such a highly developed mind as his can surely speak for himself.

JAN: Then let him speak.

KEVIN: Very well, I quote directly from the Appeals: "I speak, Americans, for your good. We must and shall be free, I say, in spite of you. You may do your best to keep us in wretchedness and misery. To enrich you and your children; but God will deliver us from under you. And woe, woe, will be to you if we have to obtain our freedom by fighting. Throw away your fears and prejudices then, and enlighten us, and treat us like men and we will like you more than we now hate you." This is the kind of appeal he made, but it appears that not many people were listening.

SHA: You know, as I sit listening to you quote from Walker's Appeals—his words sounded almost prophetic.

KEVIN: In what respect?

SHA: As I understand, the Appeals were written about two years before Nat Turner's revolt. It appears that Walker may have been able to foresee the coming of Nat's revolt—in that he raises the possibility of resorting to violence as a means of gaining freedom for Black people.

KEVIN: As to his prophecy, I cannot answer, but his writings surely reflect the wisdom of a sage. You really owe it to your education to read the Appeals.

TEACHER: I might add that David Walker's Appeals were read quite widely throughout the United States; and as a result of the very strong anti-slavery language, many whites were frightened. However, after Turner's revolt, more people in the North began to read the Appeals, and some historians feel that this helped to accelerate the development of the abolitionist movement.

KEVIN: Yes, as a matter fact, a few months before Turner's revolt, William Lloyd Garrison, a white abolitionist, began his personal protest against slavery.

JAN: Was Garrison the one who published *The Liberator*?

TEACHER: Yes, he published *The Liberator*.

SHA: What was *The Liberator*?

TEACHER: *The Liberator* was a newspaper designed to attack the evils of slavery; and subsequently called for its demise. As a result of Garrison's stand against slavery, many accused him of being a troublemaker; and at one point his printing press was destroyed by a group of irate whites. However, Garrison was determined to be heard, so he continued his fight against slavery, in spite of the attacks by angry whites.

DERRIC: I think it should be said that Garrison was certainly not acting alone in the struggle against slavery. As a matter of record, he was joined by a number of whites and Blacks; and as a result, in 1833, The American Antislavery Society came into existence.

SHA: I can very well see how Black people would put their lives on the line for their freedom; but I am wondering, what moved white people to this kind of commitment? In other words, why did they put their lives in jeopardy for the freedom of Black people?

JAN: As long as the white abolitionists were crusading against slavery in the North, do you really feel that they were putting their lives in jeopardy?

SHA: Well, of course this was dependent upon the extent of their involvement. But, I think we have to understand that there were some pro-slavery groups in the North; and some of them were very hostile toward white abolitionists, as well as Blacks. As a matter of fact, Elijah Lovejoy, a white abolitionist of Alton, Illinois, was killed by a mob of angry whites.

DERRIC: Even in such a liberal city as Boston, where the patriots so bitterly protested the tyranny of the British, an angry mob of Boston citizens, in 1835, took William Lloyd Garrison and put a rope around his neck and threatened to hang him if he didn't stop agitating against slavery.

TEDDY: Did he stop?

DERRIC: No, not until the Thirteenth Amendment was passed in 1865; of course, this was the law which freed the slaves. At this time, Garrison closed the press of *The Liberator*.

KEVIN: Before we leave the subject of white abolitionists, I think we should mention the names, James Birney, Elihu Embree, Wendell Phillips, Ralph Waldo Emerson, Henry David Thoreau, Theodore Weld, Horace Mann, and of course, John Fairfield and John Brown. All of these men, among others, joined the crusade for human freedom.

SHA: I still find it difficult to understand why men like Elijah Lovejoy and John Brown were willing to pay the supreme sacrifice for the freedom of Black people. They were blessed with the acceptable skin color of their time; and yet they would not accept this as a human reality. Well, I guess their visions were clearer than most people of their time.

TEACHER: I think you came close to answering your own question with your last statement. However, allow me to say this: Some men will be men in spite of the price they have to pay. To do otherwise, would be paying too great a price to stay alive. This principle was adequately demonstrated by Socrates of ancient Greece. It was heard resounding in our own time with the death of Dr. Martin Luther King. Both Socrates and King were warned and censured by the social and political climates of their time. But neither would accept the times in which they lived as being over and beyond severe criticism. They stood on the principles of human dignity and justice for all. However, too many people were not ready to adhere to the principles that they were teaching, and as a result, these people helped to give birth to social and political climates that would extinguish their voices. Like Socrates and King, the abolitionists knew that they were in constant danger as long as they were speaking out against slavery, but this didn't stop most of them.

DERRIC: They must have really had their heads together.

TEACHER: I must warn all of you, that as you get involved in the affairs of men, and the world, you too will find that it is not always easy to stand on sound principles, but to do otherwise is to destroy someting within you that may never be reborn.

SHA: Then, are you suggesting that it is better to die young for a good cause, than to live into old age without a cause?

TEACHER: Let us hope that in your lifetime, you won't have to make such a grave decision. But should fate decree that you do, then I hope you will find the courage to stand on human principles, whatever the cost, whatever the price.

Discussion Questions

1. What was the abolitionist movement?
2. Briefly describe the message contained in David Walker's Appeals—what was he saying to America?
3. What was *The Liberator?* Who was the publisher?
4. Name at least five abolitionists.
5. What is meant by the question, "are you suggesting that it is better to die young for a good cause, than to live into old age without a cause?"

Words you should know:

> repercussion
> analysis
> prophecy
> extinguish
> fate
> principles
> decree

Chapter 8

ABOLITIONISTS—PART II

Persons of the Dialogue: Teacher, Joseph, Jan, Teddy, Derric, Yogi, Sha, Joseph, Lynn, Kevin, Lisa and Joe.

> ... *They spent their days in the deepest kind of human struggle* ...

TEACHER: In the previous dialogue, we mentioned the fact that there were both Blacks and whites involved in the abolitionist movement, which developed in the 1830s. However, to this time, we have only mentioned one Black person who was considered to be part of the abolitionist movement. But for sure, there were others.

JOSEPH: Yes, as I recall, there were many Black abolitionists; however, when the name abolitionist is mentioned, I can think of no greater crusader for freedom and justice than Harriet Tubman.

JAN: I am glad you mentioned her—she was surely a light of hope for many Black brothers and sisters who were afraid to rise up and shake off the chains of slavery.

JOSEPH: You know, through my mind's eye, it seems as though I can see Harriet now—walking and talking with her God. And she was so sure that her God had directed her to deliver her people from the hands of their slave masters. With this in mind, sister Harriet stepped into the stream of racism and oppression and raised the banner of freedom—calling Black brothers and sisters throughout the South to follow the star.

JAN: Without a doubt, Harriet Tubman has to be one of the bravest women of all time. The thing that I admire most about Harriet is the fact that she was never content with her own escape to freedom, but she kept returning again and again to Dixie, urging and sometimes compelling Black brothers and sisters to get on the underground train and follow the star to the North.

TEDDY: I can't help but wonder, how could a woman of Harriet's stature generate so much courage and strength; especially when the odds were so great against her. She was the most wanted woman of her time, and yet she continued to go south and help others to freedom.

DERRIC: I think it can be said that when human lives are so greatly in need, as was the case of Southern slaves, the great minds don't stop to count the odds—they just accept them. Surely, Harriet Tubman fits into my category of truly great men and women.

TEACHER: Derric, you speak with the wisdom of a sage, and yet your years are so few. Tell me, how did you attain such wisdom in such a short span of time.

DERRIC: Dear teacher, if indeed it is wisdom as you say, then I must attribute that to the truly great souls that I have had the good fortune of meeting in my early years. I might add that Harriet Tubman was one of those persons who greatly inspired my quest for knowledge and a deeper understanding of my fellowman.

YOGI: But Derric, you never met Harriet Tubman.

DERRIC: No, not in the sense that you are speaking. But you forget that the printed page can be a most powerful thing. It might interest you to know that I have made many friends while plowing through the pages of a book; and so it was that

I met the great Harriet Tubman. And you know something, whenever I feel put down by the crisis of my own time, I think of Harriet's struggle, I think of Harriet's crisis, I think of Harriet's courage, and that inspires me to stand taller and drink deeper from the source of life.

TEACHER: Can you think of one thing about Harriet Tubman that stands out more than anything else?

DERRIC: That indeed would be difficult; because she possessed so many ingenious qualities. However, I remember very vividly reading about her life and how she moved in Dixie like an invisible spirit. They searched everywhere for Harriet, and she couldn't be found. But I guess I was touched deepest when I read the following statement attributed to Harriet, as she talked about her escape from slavery:

> I had reasoned dis out in my mind; there was one of two things I had a right to, liberty, or death; if I could not have one I would have de oder; for no man should take me alive; I should fight for my liberty as long as my strength lasted, and when de time come for me to go de Lord would let dem take me.[1]

TEACHER: A stirring passage for sure. If you were privileged to rewrite Harriet Tubman's epitaph, what would it be?

DERRIC: Words don't come easily—but I suppose I would say it thus: She moved with the swiftness of a mighty warrior. She fought with the strength of many men; and only death could still her voice and rest her soul. Oh—Harriet, your memory shall not fade, and your deeds shall span the ages of time.

TEACHER: In talking about Black abolitionists, we would certainly do history a great injustice if we fail to speak of Sojourner Truth. For sure, she was one of the most dedicated of all abolitionists. Who will lead us?

---

1. Sarah Bradford, *Harriet Tubman* (New York: Corinth Book Inc., 1961), p. 29.

SHA: It should be my pleaure. I was reading about Sojourner a few days ago; and I was truly fascinated by her wisdom and her personal endurance in the struggle for human rights.

TEACHER: Then, share your fascination with us.

SHA: Gladly, as many of you probably know, Sojourner was first known by the name Isabella, but for religious reasons, she assumed the name Sojourner Truth. Which, as we shall see, was a very fitting name, because she was constantly on a journey for the cause of freedom and justice for all. Like Harriet Tubman, Sojourner was a deeply religious woman, but she was very much at home in the world of protest for human rights. As a matter of fact she was the first Black woman to speak out against the inhumanity of slavery.

JAN: You mean she was crusading against slavery before Harriet Tubman?

SHA: Yes, according to my research, Sojourner is considerably older than Harriet Tubman; and was involved in very bitter protest against slavery, while Harriet Tubman was still a very young lady.

JAN: Was Sojourner also a slave?

SHA: Yes, like most Blacks of her time, she didn't escape the burden of slavery. However, she ran away from her slave master, and subsequently gained her freedom with the passage of New York's Emancipation Act of 1827.

JOSEPH: Correct me, if I am wrong; but I am of the opinion that Sojourner was the sister who experienced a sudden rebirth in her middle years, and thereafter, became a truly great servant of the people.

SHA: I think your opinion is very well documented by history. As I recall, it was in the year of 1843, when Sojourner was rapidly approaching fifty years, that she suddenly felt the glorious call to serve in the justice department of mankind. Sojourner very eloquently describes her rebirth in the following manner: "I felt so tall within—I felt as if the power of the nation was with me."

JOSEPH: After enlisting in the justice department of mankind, was she able to withstand the very rigorous demands made of her?

SHA: To that I can answer with a deep sense of pride. Sojourner was constantly speaking out against slavery, and for the rights of women. She not only matched wits with the greatest orators of her time, concerning the freedom of man, but she showed people everywhere that she could withstand the physical abuse, as well as the insulting language that was constantly directed at her from all sides.

JOSEPH: She must have been a very strong woman.

SHA: Oh, indeed she was. She was stoned and beaten, denied and rebuffed on every hand. She was thrown off of streetcars while attempting to integrate transportation facilities. However, in spite of hardships and disappointments, she held her head high, and continued to work for the abolition of slavery and the rights of all women.

LYNN: In addition to what has already been said, I should like to add that, when this country was being torn apart by the military forces of the Civil War—Sojourner was there helping to nurse Union soldiers and trying to improve sanitary conditions in the contraband camps. I think it is fair to conclude that wherever there was a problem, Sojourner was there to do her part—for sure, she believed very strongly in the brotherhood of man.

JOSEPH: After being involved in so much for so long, it would be of interest to know how she spent the latter days of her life. Did she retire after the Civil War, or did she find other burdens to bear?

SHA: I am glad you asked, and I will try to answer you. History tells us that after the Civil War, Sojourner was very tired and worn; and the scars on her body were visible proof of her most difficult and trying past. As a result, when the Civil War had ended, thinking all would be well for Black people, she attempted to settle down in Battle Creek,

Michigan, and enjoy her children and grandchildren. However, the Reconstruction years were not as kind to Black people as Sojourner and others had hoped they would be. Injustice against Black people was still rampant throughout the South —in spite of the Thirteenth, Fourteenth and Fifteenth Amendments.

JOSEPH: This must have made it very difficult for Sojourner to remain in the comfort of her Battle Creek home and enjoy the members of her family.

SHA: As a matter of fact her stay at home was very brief, and in a very short period of time, she was back on the battlefield of protest—urging Southern blacks to relocate in the North where they would have the opportunity to help themselves. When seemingly all had failed in an attempt to bring Black people into the mainstream of American life, Sojourner called on the Congress of the United States to provide money and land, so that Black people could develop their own colonies in the Wild West. This, of course, was not to be, and as a result, Sojourner and millions of other Blacks were greatly disappointed, as they stood helplessly by— watching their dreams and aspirations dwindle in the mass confusion of reconstruction and racism.

JOSEPH: I wonder, how does one find the strength and courage to go on fighting one losing battle after another.

SHA: It must have been indeed difficult for Sojourner to visualize victory in the bitter struggle of years; however, she possessed a deep and penetrating vision of the future, and she was sure that her work was not to be in vain. As a matter of fact, in the closing years of her personal struggle for human dignity and freedom, she stood in the midst of it all and proclaimed:

> The colored people will bring the whites out of Egyptian darkness into the marvelous light. The white people cannot do it, but these will. The colored people are going to be a people. Do you

think God has had them robbered and scouraged all the days of their life for nothing?

As you can see, she remained optimistic to the end.

TEACHER: It is interesting to note that when she spoke those words, she had passed into the evening of her years, and her body was constantly reminding her of that fact. Fever sores and varicose ulcers made her know that her body could no longer support the strength of her mind and the aspirations that she held for her people. Therefore, she went home to her beloved Battle Creek, and the few years left to her, she shared them with her family and friends in Battle Creek, Michigan. But for sure, the most productive years of her life were spent in the justice department of mankind. Shall we say more?

SHA: If I may, I would like to add one final statement. According to history, Sojourner was illiterate, unable to read and write. But I wonder how a formal education might have enhanced her life. She spoke with the wisdom of a sage, and her deeds were always there to sppport her words. Suffice it to say, she spent her days in the deepest kind of human struggle; and the scars on her body symbolized her quest for freedom—not just for Sojourner, I remind you, but for mankind. The light that she gave must never be extinguished.

TEACHER: Very well said. Shall we conclude our discussion of abolitionists?

KEVIN: Surely not before we pay homage to one of America's greatest freedom-fighters of the nineteenth century.

TEACHER: To whom do you refer.

KEVIN: The orator, editor, author, and without a doubt, one of the most dynamic freedom-fighters of his time—he is called by the name Frederick Douglass.

TEACHER: Oh, yes indeed, a most noble man—with a very humble origin.

Yogi: When you speak of his humble origin, to what do you allude?

Teacher: I allude to the fact that he was born in chains and reared by the lashes of his master's whip.

Yogi: Well it certainly didn't appear to affect his spirit. From the days of his youth, Frederick knew what he wanted for himself and his people; and he fought with the tenacity of a mighty warrior to achieve it.

Kevin: You are so right. I remember reading about brother Frederick sometime ago; and it's truly amazing how his masters tried by every trick that they knew to try and make him accept himself as a slave; but something within Frederick compelled him to stand up and be a man. As a result, all of the chains he wore, all of the lashes that he received, couldn't subdue his lofty spirit, nor divert his high calling to authentic manhood.

Lisa: That is indeed amazing. How long did he labor under the chains of slavery before he found a way out. Or, maybe I should ask, did he find a way out?

Kevin: Yes, I am proud to say that the day finally came when he was able to break his chains. That opportunity came when he was twenty-one years old.

Lisa: How did he manage? It must have been very difficult.

Kevin: As you know, Frederick had a very brilliant mind, and he used it to no small degree. When the time had finally come for him to shake off his chains, his friends helped him to secure a sailor's uniform, and military papers, which would identify him as a sailor. Therefore, under the disguise of a sailor, he was able to escape from his master in Maryland, and take up residence in New York. However, he later moved to Boston, where he began to gain fame as a member of the Massachusetts Anti-slavery Society.

Yogi: It must have been sweet indeed—to taste of the freedom that awaited him in the North.

Kevin: For sure—freedom is always sweet, regardless of the degree or form.

YOGI: Your meaning is not clear—will you speak further?

KEVIN: Yes, first of all Frederick was a Black man; secondly, he was a fugitive slave. As a result, when speaking to Northern whites, he was not always welcome. As a matter of fact, in Pendleton, Indiana, he was beaten severely, and left for dead. I think we should keep in mind the fact that many Northern whites did not support the cause of the abolitionist.

TEACHER: You are quite right. However, let me hasten to add, that this didn't stop most of the abolitionists; and it certainly didn't stop Frederick Douglass. Frederick was determined that he would be heard, regardless of the cost. Not only did he crusade for the abolition of slavery throughout the Northern part of the United States, but he spent two years in England, seeking support for the abolition of slavery in the United States. Upon returning to the United States in 1848, he was able to formally buy his freedom from the master that he had run away from—some ten years earlier.

JOE: I was of the opinion that Frederick was a free man after he successfully escaped from his master in Maryland, and took up residence in New York—where slavery had been abolished in 1827.

KEVIN: No, according to the Fugitive Slave Law, passed in 1793, if a slave was successful in escaping to a free state, he was to be arrested and returned to his owner. Of course, this law was not always obeyed by the authorities in the free states.

TEACHER: Very well said, Kevin. In addition to what has already been said, I should like to add that when Douglass returned from England and purchased his freedom from his master, he began to speak less and write more. As many of you may already know, before Frederick went to England, he wrote and published his autobiography. After returning from England, he began writing and publishing his own newspaper, which he called *The North Star*. Later, however, the name of the paper was changed to *The Frederick Douglass Paper*. I think it is fair to conclude that he spoke, he wrote, and he published in the name of freedom. He matched wits with the best minds of his time. After the Civil War, he held a number of very high positions in the United States Government, including that of Minister to Haiti.

JOE: Did Frederick remain loyal to the cause of freedom, after gaining fame and recognition throughout America and parts of Europe? You know it's so easy for one to look the other way when he has been successful in opening the door for himself.

TEACHER: For sure, he gained much fame and success in America and Europe, but he never lost sight of his Black brothers and sisters, who were less fortunate than he. Throughout the 1800s, and especially after the 1840s, Douglass was thought of as being the spokeman for his race. Undoubtedly, he spoke for millions of Blacks when he said:

> What I ask for the Negro is not benevolence, not pity, not sympathy, but simple justice. . . . If the Negro cannot stand on his own legs, let him fall. All I ask, give him a chance to stand on his own legs. Let him alone—if you see him on his way to school, let him alone. If you see him going to the ballot box, let him alone. If you see him going into a workshop, let him alone. If you will only untie his hands and give him a chance, I think he will live.

KEVIN: You know something—here we are, seventy-five years into the twentieth century, and some of those words spoken by brother Frederick have not yet ceased to echo.

TEACHER: How do you know?

KEVIN: I can hear them—even now.

Discuss the following:

1. The bravery of Harriet Tubman;
2. The endurance of Sojourner Truth.

3. Frederick Douglass said, "What I ask for the Negro is not benevolence, not pity, not sympathy, but simple justice." Explain.

Words you should know:

dialogue
oppression
courage
crisis
ingenious
fascinate
emancipation
rigorous
integrate
Reconstruction
aspiration
allude
autobiography

Chapter 9

THE PRELUDE TO THE CIVIL WAR

Persons of the Dialogue: Teacher, Yogi, Kevin, Regie, Teddy, Tammie, Michelle and Sha.

> ... *You cannot compromise with truth—you may postpone dealing with it for a short time—but it will surely come up again ...*

TEACHER: We have come, at last, to one of the most crucial times in American history. We have talked about slavery from its beginning in the United States. We have also talked about some of the ways in which abolitionists tried to bring about an end to slavery. It should be fairly obvious by now that nothing short of a civil war could break the chains of slavery, and provide Black people a ray of hope under the stars and stripes of the American flag.

YOGI: Am I correct in assuming that the Civil War was fought to free the slaves?

TEACHER: I can very definitely identify with your assumption. It is indeed a very common assumption made by many Americans. However, the facts of the matter tend to suggest that freeing the slaves was an effect of the Civil War and not a cause.

YOGI: Are you suggesting that the Civil War was not fought to free the slaves?

TEACHER: Yes, I am.

YOGI: Then, why was it fought?

TEACHER: In order to begin to answer that question, we must go back into the pages of history. What brave soul will lead us?

KEVIN: I think we should begin by saying that since the early 1800s, there developed some rather serious differences between different sections of the United States, and particularly, the North and the South. These differences continued to grow, until war was unavoidable.

REGIE: Yes, I was just going to say that as early as 1832, rather serious differences of opinion began to emerge between the North and the South. As a matter of fact, in 1832, South Carolina threatened to nullify a federal law on tariffs, and if necessary, withdraw from the Union if certain changes were not made in regards to tariffs.

YOGI: The threat of a state nullifying a federal law must have provoked great controversy.

REGIE: The threat not only provoked great controversy, but President Jackson quickly responded by ordering federal forts in South Carolina reinforced, and at the same time he declared he would do whatever was necessary to enforce the law. Without the clever diplomatic maneuvers of Henry Clay, a sectional collision might have taken place between the North and the South long before the 1860s. However, compromise prevailed, and physical confrontation was postponed, at least for a few years.

TEACHER: For a short time after the early 1830s, there were no major confrontations between the North and the South. However, in the late 1840s, when the abolitionist movement was gaining support, Southerners became frightened and began to press for very rigid federal laws that would protect their rights to own slaves and have them returned, should they escape to the North.

TEDDY: But they had no right to own slaves. No one has the right to own another human being.

TEACHER: I agree with you. However, the law of the land, the United States Constitution, had granted the states the right to import slaves until 1808.

KEVIN: I know what you are saying, but I would rather put it another way.

TEACHER: By all means—speak.

KEVIN: The United States Constitution speaks of slavery in the following manner: "The migration or importation of such persons as any of the states now existing shall think proper to admit, shall not be prohibited by the Congress prior to the year one thousand eight hundred and eight."

TEACHER: I see, what is your point?

KEVIN: My point is this: Rather than say the Constitution granted the states the right to import slaves until 1808, I prefer to say the Constitution denied Congress the power to stop the importation of slaves before 1808. My point is this, the flow of language is not in the affirmative, but in the negative—which leads me to believe that there was a lack of consensus among those who dealt with this very sensitive matter.

TEACHER: Without a doubt, some of the framers of the Constitution wanted to end the importation of slaves immediately. Some thought slavery shouldn't exist at all. For example, Gouverneur Morris, a Pennsylvania delegate to the Constitutional Gonvention had this to say of slavery: "I will never concur in upholding domestic slavery. It is an evil institution. It is the curse of Heaven on the states where it exists." However, the question of whether slavery should exist in the United States never really became an issue at the Convention. But, there was great debate over the question of importing slaves into the United States. Finally, compromise prevailed and, as we said earlier, the importation of slaves into the United States was allowed to go on until 1808.

TAMMIE: I thought we were discussing causes of the Civil War.

TEACHER: We are.

TAMMIE: Well, why have we proceeded to talk about the Constitution?

KEVIN: Tammie, it was never decreed that the twain should never meet. As a matter of fact, during the pre-Civil War years, interpreting the Constitution provoked very bitter debates between the North and the South.

TEACHER: For sure, we could spend a number of hours discussing slavery and the making of the Constitution. However, let us hasten on to subjects that are more relevant to the coming of the Civil War. After all, that's the question that we are trying to answer. As I was saying before we began to discuss the Constitution, the late 1840s brought the North and the South to confrontation once again.

TAMMIE: What was the matter of concern this time?

TEACHER: Well, there were two issues, and both involved the question of slavery. Who can identify these issues and discuss their implications for both sides?

REGIE: Well, at the risk of oversimplifying the matter, I will try. During the late 1840s many slaves were running away from their masters to the North. Southern slaves owners became very bitter because many Northerners would not cooperate by helping to capture the slaves and return them to Southern slave plantations. As a matter of record, many Northerners were directly involved in helping slaves to escape. As a result, Southern legislators began to press for very rigid fugitive slave laws, designed to protect their investments in slave labor. Southerners also wanted the right to extend slavery into those territories that were not yet in the Union.

KEVIN: In the meantime, and on the other hand, Northern lawmakers reacted very strongly to the South's demand for fugitive slave laws; and just as strongly against the idea of spreading slavery into territories not yet in the Union. As a result, the North and the South appeared to be extremely close to a head-on collision. But once again, Henry Clay played the role of peacemaker; and soon the tension was lessened by the Compromise of 1850. As we shall surely see, this Compromise postponed the Civil War for about ten years.

YOGI: What were the terms of the Compromise of 1850?

KEVIN: As you might suspect, the South was instrumental in getting Congress to pass a very strict fugitive slave law which would return runaway slaves to their owners. California was to enter the union as a free state. Finally, the settlers were to decide whether or not they should allow slavery in the territory acquired from Mexico. This was the essence of the Compromise of 1850.

YOGI: I would say that this Compromise was a very small consolation for Black people; and especially those on the plantations in the South. However, as I look back to the Compromise of 1850, I can see a very important principle being demonstrated.

MICHELLE: What is that?

YOGI: You cannot compromise with truth—you may postpone dealing with it for a short time—but it will surely come up again.

MICHELLE: I am not sure that I understand—perhaps, you should speak further.

TEACHER: Yes, Yogi, would you elaborate on that statement, because I think your meaning is much too important to have someone miss the point.

YOGI: Very well—I'll try. When writing the Declaration of Independence, Thomas Jefferson wrote: "We hold these truths to be self-evident; that all men are created equal; that they are endowed by their Creator with certain unalienable rights; that these are life, liberty and the pursuit of happiness." This, in my opinion, is the truth that the United States has tried to compromise from the very beginning. For example, at the Constitutional Convention, the North and the South had to compromise on the importation of slaves into the United States; they also had to compromise on the question of counting Blacks for state representation in the House of Representatives. In 1820, the United States Government had to deal with the question of slavery again, and out of this came the Missouri Compromise. In other words, there was one compromise after another, and finally in the early 1860s, the problem had to be dealt with by military confrontation.

KEVIN: Yogi, you just quoted from Jefferson's celebrated passage, "all men are created equal." I don't mean to go back to 1776, and engage you in a philosophical discussion of Jefferson's high-sounding ideals—but do you really think that he included Blacks?

YOGI: Well, since he didn't make reference to any particular race, creed or color, I have to assume that he was attempting to embrace all of mankind.

SHA: I might add that whether or not Jefferson included Blacks in his most quoted passage appears to be irrelevant. As I see it, truth is not born, but it simply exists. As to the truth of the statement "all men are created equal," it appears that this has been more than adequately demonstrated in the achievements of peoples throughout the world.

TEACHER: I see some rather puzzled faces; perhaps you should speak further.

SHA: My point is this: History is replete with the truly great accomplishments of people throughout the world, including people from varied ethnic backgrounds. In my opinion, this would tend to lend proof to the idea that, if given equal opportunities, men, regardless or their race, creed or color, can rise to common heights. This is just another way of saying that all men, generally speaking, are created equal. However, circumstances, to paraphrase Aristotle, can surely make them unequal.

TEACHER: How did we go so far afield? We were approaching the 1860s and the Civil War, and suddenly we went back almost a hundred years, and began to discuss Jefferson's ideals on the equality of man. This indeed is interesting, however; we will never get to the Civil war if we continue to discuss the implications of Jefferson's statement.

YOGI: I think I can lead us back to the subject that we were pursuing before we went off into Jeffersonian idealism.

TEACHER: Please do.

YOGI: As I recall, I was saying that you cannot compromise with truth. To that, I should like to add: You may postpone dealing with truth—but truth will surely rise again, again, and again. No compromise, however well intended, can bury truth forever. In other words, prior to 1860, the North and the South had made one compromise after another, and finally Lincoln made the astute observation that a nation can not endure half slave and half free.

TEDDY: Is it safe to conclude that Lincoln was a friend to Black people?

YOGI: I would hesitate to use the word friend. Because, to me, the word friend denotes a total acceptance of an individual or a people. I am not at all sure that this was Lincoln's point of view toward Black people. However, as a Congressman and later as President of the United States, Lincoln did take a stand against the institution of slavery.

TEDDY: To what extent did he actually try to bring an end to slavery? Of course, I am assuming that since he was against it, he tried to do something to destroy it.

YOGI: That's a very good question—I'll try to answer it to the best of my knowledge. It is a matter of record that, while serving in the United States Congress, he drafted a bill to abolish slavery in the District of Columbia. The bill, however, was defeated; but as I understand it, Lincoln continued to speak out against slavery as a thing of evil.

KEVIN: I think it should be said that while Lincoln opposed slavery on moral grounds, he did not feel that the federal government had the right to abolish slavery from the individual states.

TEDDY: Well, if this is true, why did he later free the slaves?

KEVIN: There are two things that you must keep in mind. First of all, as I said earlier, Lincoln did not believe that the federal government had the right to end slavery in the states. Secondly, he believed that no state had the right to secede or leave the Union. Therefore, he did not order the slaves freed until the Confederate states showed every intention of removing themselves permanently from the Union. By this time, of course, the North and the South had been fighting for almost two years.

TEDDY: Do I hear you saying that he freed the slaves in order to try and save the Union?

KEVIN: Precisely—the fact that he didn't order that all of the slaves be freed should prove my point.

TEDDY: What do you mean? I thought all slaves were given their freedom with the Emancipation Proclamation.

KEVIN: No, no. The Emancipation Proclamation was issued by Lincoln on January 1, 1863, and it clearly stated that slaves in those states that were in rebellion against the Union were free. However, there were slaves living in the border states, Maryland, Missouri, Kentucky, and Delaware—these states did not leave the Union, and therefore, the Emancipation Proclamation did not apply to the slaves in these states. As you shall see, freedom for all of the slaves in the United States was not accomplished until the passage of the Thirteenth Amendment, in December of 1865. By this time of course, Lincoln had met his final destiny, at the hands of an assassin.

TEACHER: For many years to come, historians will probably be debating the causes of the Civil War and the attitude that

Lincoln held in regards to freeing the slaves. However, I believe we can best summarize Lincoln's feeling about the Civil War and the abolition of slavery by referring to a statement that he made approximately a year after the war had begun. In his own words: "If I could save the Union without freeing any slave, I would do it; and if I could save it by freeing all the slaves, I would do it; and if I could save it by freeing some and leaving others alone, I would also do that. What I do about slavery, and the colored race, I do because I believe it helps to save the Union."

TEDDY: I see—saving the Union was indeed his ultimate concern, or so it seems.

TEACHER: I think that is a fair interpretation of his position.

Discussion Questions

1. What does the United States Constitution say about the importation of slaves into the United States?
2. What was the Compromise of 1850?
3. How did the Emancipation Proclamation differ from the Thirteenth Amendment? Explain.
4. What appears to be the most important reason for fighting the Civil War?
5. Briefly describe Lincoln's attitude toward slavery.

Words you should know:

> Civil War
> assumption
> confrontation
> import
> migration
> delegate
> legislator

compromise
Confederate
intepretation

Chapter 10

BLACK PEOPLE AND THE CIVIL WAR YEARS

Persons of the Dialogue: Teacher, Sha, Lynn, Derric, Regie, Kevin and Yogi.

... A great price to pay for the disappointments that followed ...

TEACHER: First of all, I should like to call your attention to the fact that Black men served in the Revolutionary War, the War of 1812, and when the Civil War began, in spite of their lowly status, they stood tall and served well, when they were finally given the opportunity.

SHA: Is it true that at the beginning of the Civil War, Blacks wanted to volunteer their services as soldiers, but were denied?

TEACHER: Yes, it is true—Blacks were not accepted as soldiers at the beginning of the Civil War.

LYNN: Why?

TEACHER: Many Union officers thought that the war would not last very long, and therefore, Black soldiers would not be needed. Secondly, some felt that the border states, Maryland,

Missouri, Delaware, and Kentucky would leave the Union if Blacks were employed as soldiers. Others were suspicious of Blacks with guns in their hand—thinking this might inspire slave insurrections.

DERRIC: Over and beyond what you have just said, I suspect that one of the real reasons that Union officials didn't want to use Black soldiers at the beginning of the war is that they didn't want to put Blacks in such a strong position for demanding their rights and their freedoms.

TEACHER: You have raised a good point, and without a doubt, this was taken into consideration by those who were determined to maintain the status quo. However, in spite of the fact that Blacks were rejected as soldiers, they still made a major contribution to the war effort in other capacities. Some worked as cooks for the troops, others served as blacksmiths, some worked as common laborers, and built fortifications for the Union army.

LYNN: You said earlier that Blacks were forbidden to serve as soldiers at the beginning of the war. Therefore, I presume that they were later accepted as soldiers. If this is true, what brought about this change of policy on the part of Union officials?

TEACHER: You are right. Later in the war, Blacks did serve as soldiers. As to the sudden change of policy by the Union government, this was brought about primarily because of the fact that the war had lasted much longer than Union officials had anticipated. Therefore, in 1862, Congress passed a series of laws which greatly affected the legal status of slaves, as well as free Blacks.

DERRIC: Yes, as I recall, the first law dealt with the absurdity of returning escaped slaves to their masters in those states that were in rebellion against the Union.

LYNN: Would you speak further, that we may grasp the whole meaning of what you are saying?

DERRIC: My meaning is not difficult to see. At the beginning of the Civil War, some union generals were returning slaves who had escaped from the rebel states. However, they later realized that they were fighting against themselves. As a result, in March of 1862, Congress passed a law forbidding union officials to return runaway slaves to their masters.

LYNN: In what sense was the Union army fighting against itself by returning the escaped slaves to their masters?

DERRIC: Do you realize that, much, if not most, of the economic strength of the South rested on the free labor of the slaves. If all of the slaves had suddenly left the plantations, it would have been extremely difficult to feed the rebel soldiers and their families. In addition, during the war, many slaves worked in the factories. Therefore, each time a slave escaped from the South, this weakened the military position of the Confederacy.

LYNN: Very well, I see what you mean.

DERRIC: Once it was determined that escaped slaves would not be returned to their masters, Union officials debated the question of whether or not runaway slaves should be free, once they had reached Union territory.

SHA: That shouldn't have caused any kind of debate, that should have been a foregone conclusion.

DERRIC: Well, it wasn't. And only an act of Congress, passed in July 1862, provided that rebel-owned slaves who had managed to escape to Union territory were to be considered captives of war, and therefore, given their freedom. At the same time, Congress passed another law which authorized the President of the United States to accept Blacks as soldiers in the United States Army.

REGIE: As a result of the above law, in September 1862, General Butler recruited the first regiment of Black soldiers into the Union Army. This was the beginning of a long list of Blacks who marched onto the battlefield during the Civil War. They joined the Union army with hope, aspirations, and great anticipations for the future. The enthusiasm, the aspirations, and the expectations of Black men, as they entered the Union Army, is probably best echoed in the words of the great abolitionist, Frederick Douglass, as he sent out the call for Blacks to volunteer their services in the Union army.

KEVIN: What did brother Frederick have to say to the brothers?

REGIE: Well, if I were talking about anyone other than Frederick Douglass, I would feel free to paraphrase their words. However, since I am talking about one of the greatest spokesman of the nineteenth century, surely he can speak for himself.

YOGI: Then, let the brother speak.

REGIE: In 1863, Frederick wrote a recruiting paper to the brothers of color, and this is what he had to say:

> The day dawns; the morning star is bright on the horizon. The iron gate of our prison stands half open. One gallant rush from the North will fling it wide open, while four million of our brothers and sisters shall march out into liberty. ... This is our golden opportunity. Let us accept it. ... Let us win for ourselves the gratitude of our country, and the best blessings of our posterity through all time.[1]

So, the call went out, and Black brothers everywhere responded. When the war had finally come to an end in April 1865, one hundred and eighty thousand Blacks had volunteered to serve in the Union army. About 68,000 of these Black brothers fell in the line of duty.

YOGI: Are you saying that 68,000 Black soldiers lost their lives in the Civil War?

REGIE: Yes, it was slightly more than that.

1. Frederick Douglass, *The Life and Times of Frederick Douglass*, revised (New York: Collier Books, 1962), p. 214.

Yogi: A great price to pay for the disappointments that followed.

Regie: I agree, but at least there was freedom on paper.

Yogi: A small consolation for a people who had given so much to a country that they wanted to be a part of.

Teacher: Before we discontinue our discussion of the Civil War years, I think we should mention the fact that, at the same time that the Civil War was going on, officials of the federal government were attempting to set up colonies in Central America, for the purpose of sending freed Blacks there to live.

Sha: Perhaps I have misunderstood you, but are you suggesting that colonies were desired in Central America for the purpose of removing Blacks from the United States?

Teacher: That is correct.

Sha: How successful was this colonizing plan?

Teacher: Let me ask you a question. How many Blacks were in the United States in 1860?

Sha: Approximately 4,500,000.

Teacher: One more question. How many Blacks are in the United States today?

Sha: The most recent population data that I saw suggest that there are more than twenty million Black people in the United States today.

Teacher: The population figure that you gave suggest that the Black population has increased more than fifteen million from 1860 to 1970. In your opinion, would these population figures suggest that the colonization plan was a success?

Sha: I think not. As a matter of fact, the evidence would point in the opposite direction.

Teacher: You have understood very well. The facts of the matter are as follows. President Lincoln was unable to secure adequate land for the establishment of a Black colony in

Central America; and as a result, the whole plan met with its demise. Of course there were some other very important reasons that the colonization plan was unsuccessful.

YOGI: Can you give some examples?

TEACHER: Sure. When Lincoln made public his colonization plan for Black people, this greatly aroused the Black population. As a result, many Black leaders wrote letters to President Lincoln denouncing the plan. Other Blacks attempted to voice their disapproval by holding protest meetings. However, the most severe protest came from those free Blacks who had managed to gain some degree of success and security. Some had managed to invest in small businesses, buy their own homes, and put a few dollars away for hard times; as a result they were violently opposed to the idea of shipping Blacks off to Central America.

DERRIC: In addition to what you have just said, many Blacks rejected the colonization plan on the grounds that the United States was the only home or country that they knew; they had given their energy, their labor and their blood for its development and survival. Therefore, many felt that no one should have the right to ship them away against their will. Of course the rest of the story is still in the making.

KEVIN: In the interest of history, I think it should be said that the idea of colonizing Blacks or shipping them out of the United States was not unique to the 1860s. As a matter of fact, as early as the 1790s and the beginning of the 1800s, both Blacks and whites were seriously discussing the return of Blacks to Africa.

REGIE: I should just like to build on what Kevin just said. As I recall, in 1811, Paul Cuffe, a black businessman from Massachusetts, sailed to Sierra Leone, a small British colony on the west coast of Africa, and while he was there, he made special arrangements to set up a Black colony. He then returned to the United States, and in 1815, he and 38 other Blacks sailed to Sierra Leone, and began to develop the little colony, which Cuffe called "The Friendly Society for American Negroes." As you might expect, Cuffe had great expectations for the little colony in Sierra Leone; however, as fate would have it, Cuffe died in 1817, and his plan for colonizing Sierra Leone was no longer pursued.

KEVIN: Before we go on, I would like to make one final observation in regards to the "Back to Africa Movement." According to my research, in 1817, this movement began to receive national recognition, under the sponsorship of the American Colonization Society. Under the leadership of men such as John C. Calhoun and Henry Clay, the society persuaded the United States Congress to contribute $100,000 for the Back to Africa Movement. As a result of the federal contributions, and gifts from other organizations, the colony of Liberia (in West Africa) came into existence in 1822. However, thirty years later, in 1852, the Black population in the United States had grown to three and a half million, but only some 8000 blacks had chosen to return to Africa.

TEACHER: By now, you can see that the colonization movement was not very popular among Black people of the United States. It really didn't matter whether it was Central America or Central Africa, the answer was the same—*No, we won't go!*

YOGI: Why do you think so few Blacks accepted the invitation to return to Africa?

TEACHER: Well, first of all, it was very expensive to travel to Africa. Secondly, many uncertainties awaited those who were brave enough to go. However, the most important reason seems to have been a lack of interest in returning to Africa. One has to understand that by the 1800s, most of the Blacks living in America were born here; and considered this their home, for better or for worse. After all, Blacks had played a most important role in the development of the United States, and it was only natural that thay wanted to share in the fruits of their labor. With this in mind more than 180,000 Black men entered the Civil War, hoping to make things right. Sixty-eight thousand of these who fought in the war gave their lives, hoping to make things right. As a result, when the Civil War finally ended in 1865, the light of hope burned high for Black people throughout the United States. And for a while, it appeared that the United States had taken a giant step forward in bringing the Black man into the mainstream of American life. However, that light which had burned so brightly at the close of the Civil War, was almost extinguished before the nineteenth century came to an end.

Discussion Questions

1. Why were Blacks denied the right to serve in the Union army at the beginning of the Civil War?
2. Why did Congress pass a law forbidding Union officials to return runaway slaves?
3. How many Blacks served in the Union Army? How many lost their lives?
4. What was the colonization plan? Why was it unsuccessful?
5. Briefly describe Paul Cuffe's African colonization plan.

Words you should know:

status quo
regiment
posterity
gallant
federal
protest
pursue

Chapter 11

THE BLACK MAN AND RECONSTRUCTION

Persons of the Dialogue: Teacher, Angie, Michelle, Darryl, Lisa, Tony and Joe.

> ... *As you cast your votes, please think of those who fought and died to make it possible* ...

TEACHER: When the Emancipation Proclamation went into effect on January 1, 1863, Black people throughout the United States sang and shouted with great expectancy. They were sure that this was the beginning of a new era for people of color. Many people gathered at public places and sang "Free at last, free at last, thank God Almighty, I'm free at last."

ANGIE: But they were not really free.

TEACHER: Well, according to the law, slaves in those states that rebelled against the Union were indeed free.

ANGIE: My point is this—freedom implies choice; and if you suddenly free a people, who have nothing, and no way of obtaining anything, what choice do they have? What freedom do they have?

MICHELLE: I agree with you, Angie—there were such limited choices for the recently freed men, that freedom was almost impossible; in spite of the Emancipation Proclamation.

TEACHER: I didn't intend to provoke a philosophical discussion on freedom; but for sure, your points are well made. However, I should remind you that when the war was finally over in 1865, there were some provisions made for widening the social and economic choices of the former slaves.

ANGIE: Like what? Did they give them forty acres and a mule? Did they provide jobs for them? Were they given protection at the ballot box?

MICHELLE: I think I can answer those questions. No, they didn't give them forty acres and a mule. However, during the Reconstruction years, Blacks did begin to actively participate in the various governments of the South, but many were kept from voting through fear and violence. As to the jobs, most Blacks were limited as to the jobs they could hold.

DARRYL: May I ask, who determined what jobs the freedmen could hold or couldn't hold?

MICHELLE: For the most part, this was determined by the government officials of the Confederate states.

DARRYL: I was of the opinion that those who fought with the Confederate states against the Union lost their right to participate in the state and local governments. In other words, they lost their right to vote.

TEACHER: You are right. But according to the plans set forth by President Johnson, Confederate soldiers were pardoned by simply pledging allegiance to the United States Government. However, the United States Congress attempted to change this by passing the Reconstruction Act of 1867. According to this Act, in order to vote, white citizens had to take a loyalty oath declaring that they had never voluntarily taken up arms against the United States Government. As a result, men who had served as officers in the Confederacy were disenfranchised, or denied the right to vote; neither could they hold any political office. At the same time, Negroes were given the right to vote and hold political offices. However, by 1869, President Johnson had pardoned most of the former Confederates; and as a result, they were now able to vote and hold political offices once again.

LISA: Well, how was it possible for Black people to gain their freedom under the political control of those men who had fought so bitterly to maintain the institution of slavery?

MICHELLE: That's just the point—they didn't gain any real degree of freedom. Because, as soon as those Confederates were pardoned and restored to political power, they began to pass laws (Jim Crow laws) designed to limit and deny Blacks their freedom. In essence, a form of slavery was legally reinstated.

TEACHER: In the interest of our discussion, I think it should be noted that during the Reconstruction Period (1865-1877) Black people did make some significant strides toward freedom. However, most of the progress made by Blacks during this period did not last very long.

DARRYL: I am not sure that I understand what you mean by the Reconstruction Period. Could you explain why, 1865 to 1877, was called the Reconstruction Period?

TEACHER: Can any of you explain the Reconstruction Period to Darryl?

TONY: I think I can turn him on.

TEACHER: OK, let's have it.

TONY: Well, you see, brother, it was like this. During the fighting of the Civil War, much of the United States was "jacked up" or, you know, just torn apart. Therefore, when the war was over in 1865, the nation had to be rebuilt or put back together. In other words, reconstructing is the same as rebuilding—so they just called it the Reconstruction Period. Get the point?

DARRYL: I hear you—very well said. A few minutes ago someone said that Black people made some significant achievements during the Reconstruction Period; but for some reason they didn't last very long. I have two questions: (1) What were the achievements? (2) Why did they last for such a short time?

TEACHER: Well, since I made the statement, I'll try and answer your questions. First of all, let me reply to your first question. In the latter part of the 1860s, the United States Congress passed a number of laws designed to give Negroes certain rights and freedoms that were denied them by the "Black Codes," or laws passed by the Confederate states during the fall and winter of 1865-66.

DARRYL: Am I correct in saying that the Black Codes were laws passed by the Confederate states for the purpose of discriminating against Black people?

TEACHER: You are correct.

DARRYL: You also said that the United States Congress passed laws giving Blacks rights and freedom that the Black Codes were denying them. Specifically, what were some of these laws?

TEACHER: For example, in 1868, the Fourteenth Amendment was passed. According to this law, all Blacks were now citizens of the United States; as well as the states in which they lived. Since Blacks were now citizens, they were supposed to have the same rights as all other citizens, regardless of race, creed or color. Also, in 1870, Congress passed the Fifteenth Amendment. This Amendment guaranteed Negroes the right to vote. In addition, Congress stated that all Confederate states had to accept the terms of these Civil Rights Amendments, before they could return to the Union.

MICHELLE: Did the Confederate states accept the terms of the Fourteenth and Fifteenth Amendments?

TEACHER: Yes—as I just said, this was the only way that these states could be re-admitted to the Union.

ANGIE: OK, let's assume that it's 1870. The Thirteenth Amendment has been passed, freeing all the slaves in the United States. The Fourteenth Amendment has been passed, giving Blacks the right of citizenship and equal protection of the law. The Fifteenth Amendment has been passed, giving Blacks the right to vote. Now, what assurance did Black people have that these rights would not be violated?

TEACHER: Good question. For sure, there were violations of the law. However, the United States Congress attempted to enforce the Civil Rights laws by sending federal troops to the Confederate states. As long as federal troops were located in the South, this gave Blacks some protection at the ballot box. As a result, Blacks began to gain some degree of political power. For example, during the Reconstruction Period, twenty-two Black men from Southern states served in the Congress of the United States. Many other Blacks held very high political offices at the state and local level.

DARRYL: Well, according to what you just said, Black people did indeed make some meaningful strides during the Reconstruction Period. However, my second question, as you may recall, was—why did these accomplishments disappear so quickly. For example, after the 1890s, there was not another Black elected to the United States Congress until 1928, when Oscar Depriest of Illinois was elected to serve in the United States House of Representatives. Why? How do you explain this?

TEACHER: First of all, I think one has to understand that the political success enjoyed by Blacks during the Reconstruction era was, for the most part, the result of federal troops being stationed in the Southern states to protect Black people's rights, including the right to vote. As long as Blacks were able to go to the polls and vote, they could elect Black men to political offices. However, by 1877, most of the federal troops had been withdrawn from the South; and as a result, Blacks no longer had federal protection; and subsequently, many of their rights were denied them once again, including the right to vote.

JOE: I think we should point out that one of the big reasons most Black people were denied the right to vote after Reconstruction in the South was because of the violent activities of the KKK.

MICHELLE: What do you mean, KKK?

JOE: Well, the proper name for the KKK is Ku Klux Klan. The Ku Klux Klan was really an organization formed by Southern whites during the Reconstruction years to prevent Negroes, carpetbaggers, and scalawags from voting and taking part in local and state government. Of course, you know they wore robes and hoods to disguise their identity.

MICHELLE: How did they operate? What kind of things did they do?

JOE: Their primary concern, of course, was to keep Blacks away from the voting polls. Therefore, they did whatever was necessary to achieve this objective. At first they tried to frighten Blacks. If this failed, they threatened them with more fearful tactics. If they were unable to frighten them away, they then resorted to violence; such as whipping, tar and feathering or even lynching.

TEACHER: Before we conclude our present dialogue, I should like to point out the fact that the activities of the Ku Klux Klan were not the only attempts by Southern whites to keep Black people from exercising their voting rights after the Civil War. For example, some states required citizens to pay a poll tax before they were able to go to the polls and vote. In addition, some states required citizens to be able to read and interpret or explain parts of the state constitution before they could vote. Perhaps one of the most ridiculous voting requirements was the implementation of the "grandfather clause." All of the above were designed primarily for the purpose of preventing Negroes from voting.

MICHELLE: I am not sure that I understand how each of the above requirements kept Blacks from voting. Will you please explain further? I am particularly interested in knowing about the "grandfather clause."

TEACHER: Very well—I shall gladly oblige. First of all, most Blacks didn't have the money to pay the poll tax, therefore, they couldn't vote. Secondly, since Blacks had just gained their freedom, most of them didn't have an education, and therefore, could not read and explain parts of the state constitution to the satisfaction of those state officials who made the rules. Finally, the "grandfather clause" declared that no person could go to the polls and vote unless his grandfather had voted or was eligible to vote in past elections. Well, you can imagine that this caused some real problems for Black citizens, because they had just gained their freedom; and their fathers, grandfathers, and great grandfathers, had been denied the right to vote. As a result, they too, were being denied the most sacred of all democratic rights, that is, the right to vote.

ANGIE: You just referred to voting as being a most sacred democratic right—why did you say that?

TEACHER: Let me try to explain. Without the right to vote, a democracy, or government by the people, is highly unlikely. I believe very strongly in a government by the people, and this kind comes only with extending the right to vote to all of the people. Besides, more than 68,000 Black men lost their lives in the Civil War; fighting for freedom and the right to go to the ballot box and cast their votes. Since the Civil War, many others have given their lives in the pursuit of freedom, and the right to be counted at the ballot box.

ANGIE: Is it your belief that we can change society through the ballot box?

TEACHER: At least we can try. We would surely do our ancestors a grave injustice if we fail to use that democratic right which they fought so long and so hard to achieve. As I said earlier, many of those Black brothers who fought so bravely in the Civil War never had the opportunity to go to the polls and cast their votes. I believe we owe it to them, if not to ourselves, to go out and vote each and every time we have the opportunity. I am still of the opinion that the right to vote is one of the most sacred of all democratic rights. Therefore, when it comes your time to help make political decisions regarding your city, state and country, don't fail to use the ballot box; and as you cast your votes, please think of those who fought so hard to make it possible.

ANGIE: I think all of us got the point.

TEACHER: I hope so—because if you didn't get the point, then I have failed you in a way that could prove very damaging to your future. Therefore, let these words go with you wherever your civic and democratic responsibilities demand your presence. Finally, as we close our dialogue on the Reconstruction years, suffice it to say that these were some difficult and trying times; and perhaps the most disappointing years of the Black experience in America. However, this was not the beginning of the Black man's struggle for freedom, justice, and equality, and as we shall see, it surely was not the end.

Discussion Questions

1. What was the Reconstruction Period? How long did it last?
2. What rights were guaranteed Blacks as a result of the Thirteenth, Fourteenth and Fifteenth Amendments?
3. How did the United States Government attempt to enforce the Civil Rights laws? Explain.
4. Give several ways in which Southerners attempted to deny Blacks the right to vote.
5. Why is voting so important to a democratic form of government?

Words you should know:

    economic
    disenfranchise
    pardon
    amendment
    democratic
    Black Codes
    creed
    local

Chapter 12

ECONOMICS, EDUCATION AND RECONSTRUCTION

Persons of the Dialogue: Teacher, Lisa, Derric, Jan, Kevin and Darryl.

> ... *After the plantation owner had taken his share, many times, there was nothing left for us* ...

TEACHER: We have talked a great deal about politics and government during the Reconstruction years. However, we have not said very much at all about economics and education for Blacks, after the Civil War.

LISA: By economics, you mean the production, distribution, and consumption of goods and services?

TEACHER: Yes, but in more simple language, I am referring to the means by which Black people earned a living for themselves and their families during the Reconstruction years.

DERRIC: The question of how Black people earned a living for themselves during the Reconstruction years is of great interest to me. Because earlier, we agreed that Blacks did not receive forty acres and a mule as suggested by Thaddeus Stevens, a Congressman from Pennsylvania. Since Blacks were denied the farm land that they needed to earn a living, and most of them did not have an education or skills, how did they survive?

TEACHER: Well, first of all, let's talk about the aid and assistance that the freedmen received from an organization set up by the federal government.

JAN: Oh, you mean the Freedmen's Bureau?

TEACHER: Are you aware of the aid and assistance that Blacks received from the Freedmen's Bureau after the Civil War?

JAN: I am not aware of the specific projects implemented by the Bureau, however, I do know that many Black people were greatly aided by this organization after the Civil War. In addition, the Freedmen's Bureau also gave assistance to poor white people who desperately needed help.

TEACHER: Can either of you state in more specific terms the kind of projects initiated by the Freedmen's Bureau, as a means of aiding the newly freed Blacks and the poor whites during the Reconstruction years?

LISA: According to my research, the Freedmen's Bureau was set up in March of 1865, and one of its greatest tasks was to train freedmen for job opportunities. The Bureau also attempted to negotiate labor contracts which would help the freedmen to earn a decent salary. However, the problem of unemployment was so widespread among the recently freed Blacks, that many Blacks were not aided at all by the efforts of the Freedmen's Bureau.

DERRIC: In addition to helping people find jobs, the Bureau also provided food, clothing and medical care for the newly freed Blacks, as well as the poor whites. However, according to my research, the Bureau's greatest contribution was in the area of education. It is estimated that nearly 250,000 Blacks received some formal education as a result of the efforts of the Freedmen's Bureau. In order to reach such a large number of people, from 1865 to 1872, the Freedmen's Bureau organized more than 4000 schools throughout the South. In spite of the educational efforts of the Freedmen's Bureau, most of the four million former slaves did not receive any formal education.

JAN: Am I correct in assuming that since most Blacks were unable to get an education, or some kind of meaningful training, they were still, for the most part, dependent upon white plantation owners?

TEACHER: I would say that you have made a very good observation; and we shall begin to understand this more clearly as we talk about the sharecropping system, which spread very rapidly throughout the South after the Civil War. Perhaps some of you would like to lead us in a discussion of the sharecropping system, before we go further.

KEVIN: Well, I guess I should be an expert on the sharecropping system, because I have heard my grandfather speak of this system many, many times. As a matter of fact, if anyone so much as mentions the South in the presence of my grandfather, he will usually end up giving a long lecture on tenant farming and sharecropping. One did not have to listen to him very long before he convinced you that the sharecropping system was not too far removed from slavery.

DARRYL: Was your grandfather a history teacher?

KEVIN: No—not in the formal sense of the word. You see, he gained his knowledge from real life experiences, or you might say, on-the-job training. In other words, my grandfather was a sharecropper for some forty years. Therefore, I think he earned the right to speak as an authority on the subject. However, sometimes I wish he wasn't so aware of the struggles of our past.

TEACHER: Why?

KEVIN: Because every time I vaguely mention dropping out of school, he gives me a long lecture about the difficult and trying times that he had supporting his family while working as a sharecropper. He reminds me constantly that without an education my future may be as difficult as his past. I must confess that his lectures have greatly encouraged me to stay in school and learn as much as I can. However, sometimes I pretend that I am not listening to what he says, but I am sure that the wisdom of his years lets him know that he's being heard—besides, sometimes I tell him so.

TEACHER: It must be beautiful indeed to hear history from someone who helped to make it. However, for the benefit of those who didn't have that opportunity, will you share your knowledge with us?

KEVIN: Well, simply put, sharecropping is the process by which farmers pay part of their crop as rent for the land they farm.

TEACHER: Can you say more about how the system worked, and the reason for its existence?

KEVIN: OK, I will try. In a previous dialogue, we said that after the Civil War slavery was supposed to be a thing of the past. In other words, the Thirteenth Amendment made it unlawful to enslave another human being in the United States. Now, as a result of the Civil War, approximately four million Blacks were supposed to have been freed from their masters and the plantation system. However, most of these freedmen had been denied education and job skills; and therefore, were not prepared to earn a living for themselves and their families. The one thing that most freedmen knew how to do best was till the soil, but as you will surely recall, the freedmen were not given forty acres and a mule, as suggested by some Northern Congressmen. As a result, they lost the opportunity to become independent of their old plantation masters.

DERRIC: Very well, Kevin, I hear what you are saying—but you still didn't explain sharecropping to the extent that we know exactly what was going on. Will you speak further?

KEVIN: OK, I'll try and run it down to you. You see, after the Civil War, many Southern planters were allowed to keep their plantations. However, since slavery had been abolished by the Emancipation Proclamation and the Thirteenth Amendment, there was no labor force to cultivate the land for the plantation owners. Therefore, the plantation owners had to devise some means of getting the freedmen to work their land, or else most of the land would not be cultivated.

DERRIC: All right, so far, so good—but in very specific terms, how did the sharecropping system work?

KEVIN: OK, let me explain. The plantation owners divided their plantations into small units or tracts of land; they then made agreements with Black families to farm the land. Each family was usually assigned a certain acreage of land to cultivate and harvest. Once the crop was harvested, the sharecroppers paid their rent to the plantation owner by giving him part of their crops. This is the way the sharecropping system was supposed to work.

DERRIC: In other words, if a family produced twenty bales of cotton, the land owner was to get approximately ten bales?

KEVIN: For the most part you are right—however, some land owners required more than half of the crop as their share. And according to my grandfather, after the plantation owners had taken their share, many times there was nothing left for the sharecropper and his family. They simply had to survive as best they could.

Discussion Questions

1. What was the Freedmen's Bureau? How did it help Black people?
2. Describe the sharecropping system. Why did it grow so rapidly after the Civil War?
3. After the Civil War, most Blacks were still dependent on the white plantation owners for their survival? Why? Explain.

Words you should know:

skills
initiate

observation
cultivate
negotiate
consumption
congressman
politics

Chapter 13

BLACK PEOPLE AND THE SUPREME COURT

Persons of the Dialogue: Teacher, Sha, Derric, Anton, Lynn and Lisa.

> ... *After the seeds of justice were planted with the passage of the Thirteenth, Fourteenth and Fifteenth Amendments, these seeds almost died before they took root in the legal system of the United States* ...

In the late 1850s, when the North and South seemed destined to settle their differences on the battlefield, the Supreme Court was asked to rule on the legal status of a slave who had lived in free territory with his master for four years. This ruling, as we shall see, had far-reaching implications for Black people, both free and slave, throughout the United States.

SHA: Oh, you mean the Dred Scott Case of 1858?

TEACHER: Exactly. Were you one of the students who did research on this case?

SHA: Yes, and I found the decision of the Supreme Court rather disturbing.

TEACHER: Well, before you comment on the decision reached by the Court, perhaps you should explain to the class what the Dred Scott Case was all about.

SHA: It's a long story, but I'll try and make it as brief as I can. First of all, Dred Scott was a slave who was owned by a slave holder in the state of Missouri. Dred Scott's master took him out of the slave state of Missouri and into free territory in the North. Here in the free territory of the North, Dred Scott lived with his master for four years. After living four years in free territory, Scott's master took him back to the slave state of Missouri. Upon returning to Missouri, Dred Scott thought that he should be given his freedom because he had lived in free territory for four years. Sympathizing with his situation, a number of his friends helped him to develop his case, and finally present it to the Supreme Court.

DERRIC: Did the Court rule in Scott's favor, or did they attempt to maintain the status quo?

SHA: Well, when the case finally reached the Supreme Court, the court ruled that Dred Scott was not a citizen of the United States and therefore had no right to sue in a court of law. As a result, according to the court ruling, Scott was still a slave and subsequently the property of his master. As if that was not enough, Chief Justice Taney and the Court ruled that citizenship of the United States was not only denied to Dred Scott, but other Black people as well. According to the court ruling, no Black person, whether free or slave, was entitled to become a citizen of the United States.

ANTON: This decision must have greatly diminished the hopes and aspirations of Black people throughout the United States.

SHA: Indeed it did—but as fate would have it, this was not to be the final word. As a matter of fact, this decision greatly increased the political differences between the North and the South, and to some extent, it accelerated the coming of the Civil War.

LYNN: I think it should be said that despite the Dred Scott decision denying Blacks the right of citizenship, this decision was not always recognized by the State Department. For example, in 1861, Henry Highland Garnet, a black man, was issued a passport to travel abroad, and this passport clearly stated that Garnet was a citizen of the United States.

TEACHER: All of this seems to point up the social, Constitutional, and political confusion which had been developing between the North and the South, at least since the Missouri Compromise of 1820.

LYNN: Are you suggesting that the Supreme Court's decision, in the Dred Scott Case, was politically motivated?

TEACHER: Well, I didn't intend to suggest that at all. However, I will say that, in my opinion, legal interpretations of the law, including the Constitution, are not always free of social and political considerations, and I believe this includes some of the decisions that have been handed down by the Supreme Court.

LYNN: I agree. However, the one thing that bothered me most about the Dred Scott Case, is the fact that a human being could be considered a mere piece of *property* by the highest court in the land.

SHA: I hear you—however, one does derive some degree of satisfaction from the fact that this decision did not have a very long life; at least in theory.

LYNN: You mean?

SHA: I mean the Dred Scott decision was completely overturned with the passage of the Thirteenth and Fourteenth Amendments, which abolished slavery and granted citizenship to Black people throughout the United States. Of course, this was not to be until this country had been torn apart by the military forces of the Civil War.

TEACHER: It is indeed unfortunate that the Civil War had to come upon this country before the seeds of justice could be planted within the hallowed walls of our federal and state court systems—but that's the way it was, a grim fact that is yet casting shadows over our legal system, wherever justice is actively pursued.

DERRIC: In addition to what you have just said, after the seeds of justice were planted with the passage of the Thirteenth, Fourteenth, and Fifteenth Amendments, these seeds almost died before they took root in the legal system of the United States. As a matter of fact, before the nineteenth century came to a close, the Supreme Court handed down another decision which had far-reaching consequences for Black people throughout the United States. As a matter of record, in 1896, the Supreme Court handed down the decision on the Plessy *vs.* Ferguson Case. This decision stood much longer, and its effects may have been much more detrimental to Blacks than the Dred Scott Decision.

LYNN: In what sense?

TEACHER: Derric, before you discuss the implications of Plessy *vs.* Ferguson, I think you should give us some background to the case.

DERRIC: You mean I should tell you what the case was about?

TEACHER: Yes, I don't think it is fair to assume that all of us are knowledgeable about the Plessy *vs.* Ferguson Case.

DERRIC: OK, I'll try and relate my findings as best I can. According to my research, the Plessy *vs.* Ferguson Case came before the Supreme Court in 1896. This case involved a Louisiana Jim Crow law, which called for separate railroad facilities for Blacks and whites.

ANTON: In other words, you are saying that white people didn't want Black people sharing public transportation facilities with them?

DERRIC: Oh, how did you guess?

ANTON: Well, let's just say that I had a brainstorm, and all of my intuitive powers were suddenly activated. You know, something like that.

DERRIC: It doesn't surprise me that you have a sense of humor. However, let's return to the case at point—Plessy *vs.* Ferguson, in 1896. As I said earlier, this case raised the question of whether or not Black people had the right to share public railroad facilities with white people. In other words, Plessy was a Black man, who insisted on riding in the same coach that white people rode in. When he was denied this opportunity, he felt that his Constitutional rights had been violated; and as a result, he took his case to the courts.

LYNN: I hope the courts were more kind to Plessy than they were to Dred Scott.

DERRIC: Well, hear the facts of the case, and then draw your own conclusions.

LYNN: I am tempted to draw my conclusions before I hear the facts.

DERRIC: That would be a purely emotional response, violating the laws of academic inquiry. Such nonsense, we cannot tolerate.

LYNN: You know something, Derric, those words sound very strange coming from you. You make it sound as though we come from completely different backgrounds, with completely different experiences. However, lest I be charged with committing some grave academic error, I will listen to your facts, before I draw my conclusions.

DERRIC: Very well, my dear, you have made a wise choice. The facts of the case are as follows: In 1896, the Plessy *vs.* Ferguson case came before the United States Supreme Court. After hearing the case, the court, under the leadership of Chief Justice Brown, ruled that Plessy's Constitutional rights had not been violated as a result of the segregated railroad accommodations to which he had been subjected. The Court said that there was nothing wrong with separating Blacks and whites, as long as both were provided equal facilities.

LISA: So that's where the "separate but equal doctrine" enters American history?

DERRIC: Precisely.

LISA: I am in disagreement with that decision.

DERRIC: So was Justice Harlan—however, the decision and all of its implications stood between Black people and justice for more than a half century.

LISA: Who was Justice Harlan?

DERRIC: He was a Supreme Court justice who wrote the dissenting opinion in the Plessy *vs.* Ferguson Case. I might add that he stood alone in his dissent.

ANTON: On what grounds did he stand?

DERRIC: I will let him speak to that. In his own words: "Our Constitution is color-blind, and neither knows nor tolerates classes among citizens. In respect of civil rights, all citizens are equal before the law." It appears that he saw and recognized the unspoken language of that decision, and as a result, conscience dictated that he speak out against it.

ANTON: I would say that he was before his time.

DERRIC: Yes, as a matter of fact, I would say that he was about sixty years ahead of his time.

ANTON: Why did you say sixty years?

DERRIC: As you shall see, it wasn't until 1954, in Brown *vs.* Board of Education, that the Supreme Court began to move in the direction suggested by Justice Harlan sixty years earlier.

ANTON: OK, I see your point very clearly—however, before we go further, I would like to ask Lisa a question. Lisa, earlier you said that you were in disagreement with the Plessy *vs.* Ferguson decision, so am I, but I would like to know more specifically, why you are in disagreement with this decision?

LISA: Well, my disagreement was not so much with the "separate but equal decision," but, as I look back through the pages of history, I can see very clearly how this decision led to a kind of caste system which always separated Blacks from whites, but almost never provided them with equal public facilities and equal protection under the law of the land. I am sure that Justice Harlan saw this injustice being built into the legal system, and of course he spoke out against it in no uncertain terms. In other words, the Plessy *vs*. Ferguson decision prepared the way for Southerners to subject Blacks to second-class citizenship, under the guise of "separate but equal." Yes, I agree with Justice Harlan that this decision was hostile to both the spirit and the letter of the Constitution. Finally, I think one does not have to be a legal analyst to see how deeply the Supreme Court has entered into the history of this country, and particularly the lives of Black people.

LYNN: As I look back to the Plessy *vs*. Ferguson decision, I cannot help but think that we would be much closer to racial harmony and equality, here in the 1970s, if we had not been forced to live with the Plessy *vs*. Ferguson decision for almost sixty years.

DERRIC: I am in complete agreement with you. However, it does little good to lament over what might have been; clearly, our challenge is to squeeze the greatest amount of justice out of the present situation.

ANTON: I think it should be said that however dark the years following the Plessy *vs*. Ferguson decision, in 1954, a ray of light shone within the chambers of the Supreme Court, and the historical forces of justice were no longer to be denied—at least in theory.

DARRYL: Pardon my ignorance, but apparently I have not read as widely as some of you have, and as a result, I don't understand some of the things to which you have alluded. For example, someone mentioned living with the Plessy *vs*. Ferguson decision for sixty years, and then someone made mention of the Brown *vs*. Board of Education decision which was handed down by the Supreme Court in 1954. I assume that there is a historical connection between these two Supreme Court decisions, but I am not sure that I know how these cases are historically related to each other. I wish someone would comment on this.

TEACHER: Thanks, Darryl, I am glad you made that observation. Because we have not shown the relationship between Plessy *vs.* Ferguson and Brown *vs.* Board of Education.

DERRIC: I am sorry—I just assumed that the relationship was obvious.

TEACHER: As researcher and reporter, you must not assume anything. Your job is to gather the facts, and report them as clearly and completely as you can. That indeed is the mark of a serious student.

DERRIC: I guess I am guilty of committing a grave academic error—therefore, I offer my sincere apology.

TEACHER: With that kind of apology, we have no choice but to forgive you.

DERRIC: Ok, back to Darryl's question on the historical relationship between Plessy *vs.* Ferguson and Brown *vs.* Board of Education. Earlier, we said that the Plessy *vs.* Ferguson case involved a "Jim Crow" law in Louisiana. We also said that this law required separate coaches for Blacks and whites riding the train within the state of Louisiana. Plessy, a Black man, thought that this law violated his Constitutional rights. Therefore, Plessy's case finally reached the Supreme Court; and in 1896, the Court ruled that it was legal for a state to have laws requiring separate public facilities for Blacks and whites, as long as these facilities were equal. Again, while public facilities in the South were always separate, they were almost never equal.

DARRYL: This much I understand, however where does Brown *vs.* Board of Education enter into all of what you have been saying about segregation in public places?

DERRIC: I was just going to get to that. By 1950, there were many questions being raised in regards to whether or not forced segregation in public schools was legal, or Constitutional. The NAACP, an organization designed to help Black people gain their rights, was particularly interested in this question. As a result, in 1952, the NAACP., was successful in bringing before the Supreme Court five cases involving segregation in public schools. Together, all of these five cases were called Brown *vs*. Board of Education. Two years later, in 1954, the Supreme Court finally handed down its decision on Brown *vs* Board of Education.

DARRYL: And what did they say this time?

DERRIC: The Court ruled that separate educational facilities were inherently unequal; and therefore, unconstitutional because they denied Negro children equal protection of the law which is guaranteed by the Fourteenth Amendment. This decision reversed the Plessy *vs*. Ferguson decision which had stood for sixty years.

DARRYL: In other words, it took the Supreme Court sixty years to reach the conclusion that segregation was wrong.

DERRIC: In essence—you are right.

LISA: I think it should be said here, that the Brown *vs*. Board of Education decision of 1954, not only declared forced segregation in public schools unconstitutional, or unlawful, but at the same time, this decision set in motion a series of laws which were designed to do away with segregation in other public places, as well as schools. Some of the public places that were later affected by this decision were golf courses, swimming pools, athletic fields and theaters. Obviously, this was the beginning of a new era in the struggle for civil rights and equal opportunities for Black people. And as you might suspect, twenty years later, the struggle is still very much alive.

TEACHER: As we come to the close of our dialogue on the Black man and the Supreme Court, you should be aware of the fact that we have not discussed many Supreme Court decisions that have directly and indirectly affected the lives of Black people in the Unites States. However, I will leave it to you to ask further questions, and seek additional answers. But you must always remember—answers don't necessarily come easily, but often require much effort, hard work, and perhaps most of all, endurance.

Discussion Questions

1. Who was Dred Scott?
2. How did the Supreme Court rule on the Dred Scott Case? Explain.
3. Describe the Plessy *vs.* Ferguson Case. How did this case affect the lives of Black people?
4. Justice Harlan disagreed with the decision reached by the Supreme Court in Plessy *vs.* Ferguson. Why? Explain.
5. Describe the Brown *vs.* Board of Education case. What was the Supreme Court's decision in this case? How did this case affect the lives of Black people in the United States? Explain.

Words you should know:

detrimental
academic
segregate
Supreme Court
unconstitutional
era
reverse
Jim Crow laws
passport
diminish

Chapter 14

A FINAL WORD

Persons of the Dialogue: Teacher, Sha, Jan, Teddy, Joseph, Darryl, Joe, Tony, Yogi, Tammie, Angie, Michelle, Kevin, Lisa, Regie, Lynn, Derric and Anton.

> *... There is justice in the universe, and your job is to plant it in the minds of men ...*

TEACHER: As I look back over the past series of dialogues, I urge you all to keep in mind the fact that we have only just begun to explore the Black experience in America. Obviously, we have not said a great deal that needs to be said; and I am sure that some of our dialogues were terminated before we adequately answered some of the questions that we raised. However, you should be aware of the fact that asking the intelligent question has its own virtue—which is often independent of the answers we seek. As you young people avail yourselves of educational experiences in the future, you will surely ask questions to which there are no immediate answers. But for sure, to ask the right question at the right time is indeed an educational experience worthy to be shared. Speaking of sharing, before we conclude our dialogues on the Black experience in America, I should like for each of you to briefly share with all of us what you have heard, what you have seen, and most of all, what you are feeling now, as you look back upon the Black man's experience in America. Who will lead us?

SHA: As I see it, looking to our past may very well inspire a vision for the future.

JAN: I can see more clearly now, how yesterday is a part of today, today is a part of tomorrow, and tomorrow is a part of eternity. That, my friends, is all I can see.

TEDDY: When history lives, it conveys the deep sentiments of a people. Those sentiments are deepened when they reflect the struggles and the hardships of an oppressed people. That's what I felt as we talked about the Black experience in America.

JOSEPH: My quest for knowledge has been greatly intensified, and as I see it, the search has just begun.

DARRYL: At last I have touched the source of my heritage, and nobody can ever change that. I guess I am really trying to say that I have discovered something of value.

JOE: Another step in the path of knowledge—sometimes lonely, but always rewarding.

TONY: It is much easier to be Black in America when you understand from whence you have come.

YOGI: It is indeed reassuring to know that the spirit of man can rise above racism. This spirit was vividly illustrated by the lives of men like Elijah Lovejoy, Levi Coffin and William Lloyd Garrison. It appears that some men never rise above their own shadows—while others never descend to this level of thinking.

TAMMIE: In addition to what Yogi just said, as the dialogues unfolded, I was deeply impressed by the fact that there were some whites who chose to stand with Blacks in the struggle for freedom. As someone said earlier, it is refreshing to know that some men will be men, regardless of the price they have to pay.

ANGIE: As I experienced the forces of my history beating upon the walls of my mind, I tried to make myself believe that it was all one bad dream. I thought surely no people could have endured so much for so long. However, reality prevailed, and I was forced to accept the facts of my past in American history. As bitter as it was, I no longer wish to forget; instead, I take pride in the fact that my people have contributed so much under such difficult and trying circumstances. This, to me, is the sign of a truly great people.

MICHELLE: To know your history is to know your strength. Without a knowledge of your past, there is very little to build on. If we fail to build on the strengths of our past, we may perish in the political whirlwinds of tomorrow.

KEVIN: As I see it, the resiliency of the Black man's spirit is probably one of his greatest assets. When the winds of racism and injustice blew heavily upon him, he simply recoiled—to spring forth again, again, and even again.

LISA: The quest for freedom is indeed a powerful thing. This is unbelievably true, when I consider the struggle of my ancestors.

REGIE: As the dialogues were developing, I felt the pulse of freedom's beat—it was warm, but restless.

LYNN: At this point, it appears that the whole struggle of the Black man is before my very eyes. However, I bear no tears of my past. I bear no sorrow of my past. I simply look forward to the birth of a new day; when all men can enter into the mainstream of American life without reference to race, creed or color. As a young person, I hope I can help to give birth to that moment in our history.

TEACHER: As I sat listening to each of you, I was convinced that all of you will become carpenters of tomorrow's world. Therefore, I say to you all, when you are sure that your vision is clear—go forth and build a better world. You should always remember, there is justice in the universe, and your job is to plant it in the minds of men.

DERRIC: You have charged us with a great responsibility, I hope we can find the way.

ANTON: I believe I reflect the thinking of all of us, when I say young people of the world join us in building a better world in which to live. And as we build, we must be careful to recognize the wisdom of the past, for that is the glue that will hold our future together. However, at the same time, we must bury, once and for all, those things that continue to separate man from man. When reason and wisdom have prevailed, we will surely understand that *wars, bombs* and *racism,* have no place in the affairs of men—they belong to a lesser species.

TEACHER: I hope the world is listening.